P9-CCF-363

DUE DATE

Nov 22			
FEB 23			
MAY 03			
JUL 23 1994			

248.4
HIN
#6933

Hinson, William H.
Reshaping the inner
you.

$13.95

DATE

248.4
HIN
#6933

Hinson, William H.
Reshaping the inner you.

$13.95

CHRIST UNITED METHODIST CHURCH
4488 POPLAR AVENUE
MEMPHIS, TENNESSEE 38117

Reshaping the Inner You

Being Transformed by the
Power of God's Love

Other Books by William H. Hinson

Solid Living in a Shattered World
A Place to Dig In

248.4
HIN

RESHAPING
THE INNER YOU

Being Transformed by
the Power of God's Love

William H. Hinson

6933

CHRIST UNITED METHODIST CHURCH
4488 POPLAR AVENUE
MEMPHIS, TENNESSEE 38117

1817

Harper & Row, Publishers, San Francisco

Cambridge, Hagerstown, New York, Philadelphia, Washington
London, Mexico City, São Paulo, Singapore, Sydney

Quotations from the Bible in this book are from the Revised Standard Version, copyrighted 1946, 1952, 1971 by the Division of Christian Education of the National Council of Churches of Christ in the U.S.A.; the New International Version, copyright ©1973, 1978, 1984 International Bible Society; and the King James Version.

Lines from the hymn "I Won't Have to Cross Jordan Alone," copyright ©1934 Stamps-Baxter Music Company. Used by permission.

RESHAPING THE INNER YOU: *Being Transformed by the Power of God's Love.* Copyright © 1988 by William H. Hinson. All rights reserved. Printed in the United States of America. No part of this book may be used or reproduced in any manner whatsoever without written permission except in the case of brief quotations embodied in critical articles and reviews. For information address Harper & Row, Publishers, Inc., 10 East 53rd Street, New York, NY 10022. Published simultaneously in Canada by Fitzhenry & Whiteside, Limited, Toronto.

FIRST EDITION

Library of Congress Cataloging-in-Publication Data

Hinson, William H.,
    Reshaping the inner you.

    1. Christian life—Methodist authors.
I. Title.
BV4501.2.H522   1988   248.4'876   87–46211
ISBN 0–06–063933–4

88 89 90 91 92 RRD 10 9 8 7 6 5 4 3 2 1

We are the clay, and thou art our potter;
we are all the work of thy hand.

—ISAIAH 64:8

To

Charles Milton Hinson, Sr.
(August 21, 1901–July 19, 1960)

and

John Alfred Laird
(March 15, 1910–February 11, 1968)

Contents

Preface

Our world is into "shaping." Many of us jog, swim, lift weights, or take aerobic exercise classes in an effort to shape ourselves more perfectly. We try to build strong relationships; we set high financial and educational goals; we rigorously schedule our time, hoping to fashion a brighter future for ourselves and our children.

Something vital is missing in this emphasis on mastering all these external trappings of life. For we know that dreams and plans have a way of slipping through our fingers. We want to be better, happier people—but relationships go awry; frustrations and fears block our path; depression fogs the view; temptations lure us in wrong directions; accidents, sickness, or suffering eclipse our hopes for a happy, fulfilled life.

What are we to do if these things befall us?

I have learned, in my years as a pastor and through personal experience, that we can allow the hard times to steal all of life's rich meaning, or we can enter into a renewing process that will reshape us from the inside out. This is not a naive statement. It is based on my slow but steady discovery that the steadfast love of God never fails. At no time was that love more evident than when he sent his own son, Jesus Christ, to walk earth's dusty roads, experiencing all the highs and lows that life throws at every one of us.

This book had its beginning with my desire to make the reality of Jesus' incarnation more real to the people who are struggling with difficulties that seem too much for them. What I want to say, in the broadest sense, is that in the middle of turbulent, sometimes discouraging, times God has not abandoned us. He is working in the lives of people and in the very events that shape and mold our world.

What we need to gain, primarily, is the right perspective, a quality of spiritual sensitivity. Then we can begin to see an extraordinary power at work in the ordinary occurrences of our lives. We can be saved from cynicism and despair by the quiet realization that our Creator could never abandon his highest creation. Not only that, but he has also sent his son to lead and direct us.

As I have learned to walk in his path, I have made some foundational discoveries. One is that a large portion of our uneasiness and anxiety has its origin in a fear of the unknown. If, however, we are enabled through faith to see that the One who comes to us comes to show us a "known way," much of the dread is taken from our darkness. Like the ancient people who followed a cloud by day and a pillar of fire by night, we find, to our great joy, that God does not set us out to walk through the wilderness alone, but he always goes before us. The rough and untried places are not so intimidating after we learn that the great Pioneer of our faith has preceded us into every place where we ourselves must go.

And there is an even deeper dimension. Our faithful guide not only goes with us and before us in our outward journey, but he also shares the highs and lows of our emotional lives—our inner beings. Aloneness in our inner self can be more painful than exterior loneliness. In the unseen world of our emotions we sometimes have great difficulty owning a feeling—that is, it is hard to acknowledge we feel a certain way because we think it impossible that anyone else has ever felt the same. How wonderful and freeing it is to learn that our Lord felt fear, temptation, irritation, loneliness. He offers us not only a way to deal with our frightening feelings, but also the special companionship of One who has been there. For whatever you are feeling, Christ has felt.

Also, I have discovered that the presence of our Guide is not dependent upon our performance. This makes faith relevant and keeps our hope alive, because we can also grow beyond the place where we merely celebrate our successes—we can claim our failures, learning and being changed by them. This freedom comes when we find that the One who promises never to leave or forsake us was also wounded. Like us, he knew exasperation and discouragement. He does not walk with us as a "quality-control engineer," but as a loving parent. He is disappointed by our refusal to search for life in the right places, but he is for us with a determination that will stand the test of time. The potter does not abandon the clay because some imperfection emerges.

What about when really bad things happen? When our spouse develops cancer? When we lose our job? When we disappoint our friends and family? When we see failure and weakness in ourselves? These are the turning points when we ask God, "Why? How could this happen to me?" In these pivotal times, we search for meaning. Where is God in the middle of all this? This book is about seeing God in the Scriptures, in the lives of ordinary people, and in your own circumstances.

Not long ago, a young friend of mine swam up from unconciousness in the intensive care unit of a hospital. Even as she came out from under the anesthetic following her first surgery for cancer, she knew that this was only the first step in what would be a long series of painful procedures in her battle against the disease. It might have been a moment of despair.

But as she woke, she sensed an unnatural brightness in the room. And she heard an unmistakable voice in the stillness of her soul, saying, "Trust me, and I'll take care of you."

My friend's fight against cancer continues—and yet she is one of the strongest, most triumphant people I have ever met.

Life in a fallen, imperfect world is full of trouble. If we would deepen in our spiritual strength, we must let go of the notion that God has sent the trouble to bruise or chastise us. We must be willing to let him "sanctify our distress," entering into the process by which difficulties make us stronger, happier people.

Whether it is a malignancy, the blight of a beastly temper or a foul disposition, a choking fear or a nameless dread, God can use our struggles—*if we will trust him*—to shape us into the people we were created to become.

Earlier, I mentioned the outward shaping that many are into today. We are reinforced in our determination to be in good physical condition by the advice of medical science and by the Scriptures. In the Apostle Paul's first letter to Timothy, we read that "bodily training is of some value. . . ." In the same passage, however, we are admonished that "godliness is of value in every way, as it holds promise for the present life and also for the life to come" (1 Timothy 4:8).

My hope is that this book will enable you to see that God is working to mold you into the person you yearn to become. Like a skilled and determined potter, our God can take the raw materials of our lives in his hands, if we will let him, and reshape our inner beings. Reshaped and redirected by his gentle power and love, we will with great joy begin to live the abundant life that is our gift.

Acknowledgments

I am grateful to David Hazard who, with real skill and sensitivity, has transposed a great deal of verbal material into an easy-to-read literary form.

I am grateful to John Shopp, my editor, for his encouragement and his creative ideas.

To my former secretary, Gail Keller, I am grateful for the endless and patient hours of typing necessary to the preparation of this manuscript.

In all of my ministry, whether preaching or writing, I am supported and strengthened by my wife, Jean. For her and the gift of our life together, I am most grateful.

1. When the Heat Is On
Not Being Afraid of the Little Things

On a bleak, cold December night in 1983, the phone woke me from a sound sleep. Reaching for the receiver, I saw by the bedside clock that it was 3:30 A.M.

A voice at the other end of the line delivered the shocking news. "You'd better come quickly. Your church is on fire."

As if in a fog, I drove cautiously along the icy streets of Houston in the direction of the church. The city was having one of the worst winters in its history. Nighttime temperatures were well below freezing. It was just two days after Christmas and lights from the downtown stores reflected on the glazed pavement.

Turning onto Main Street, my heart sank. Fire trucks were parked at angles in the street, and men were running with hoses. The historic First Methodist Church was engulfed in fire. I'd come to serve this church just six months before, following in the footsteps of the well-known and well-loved Dr. Charles Allen. Stepping out of my car, I saw flames leaping through a hole where there had been a stained-glass window.

Numb with disbelief, I stepped inside the sanctuary door to watch as firemen fought to bring the blaze under control. A gaping hole in the sanctuary floor had opened, and I could look down into the lower levels of the building. Even as I looked on, the massive pipes of our organ, which had been called "a masterpiece," caved in on themselves.

Just before I turned away from that fiery disaster, something caught my eye.

In the back of the sanctuary, I saw a banner we had used on All Saints Sunday. Lit by the light of flames, it proclaimed the great promise of Romans 8: "Nothing can separate us from the love of God in Christ Jesus."

During the coming months, I held tightly to that promise amid a hail of questions and challenges.

Repairs to our building would cost millions of dollars. We were forced to worship in the ballroom of a nearby hotel while the work went on, causing some marginal members to abandon us for other churches. Once we got back into the sanctuary, others left because they didn't want to sit on folding chairs for five months while we waited for the new pews to come in.

One difficulty for me was the fact that I was following in the footsteps of a legend. The jury was still out regarding the question of whether I could fill the shoes of Charles Allen. One irate individual wrote to a Houston paper and complained, "That fire wouldn't have happened if Dr. Allen was still pastor."

I was even being blamed for the fire! Why was all this happening?

To tell you the truth, I never did find concrete answers to my questions—not even the true cause of the fire. Instead, I had to trust in the simple yet resounding assurance of God's love, right in the midst of disaster. Those words from Romans 8 gave me a certain strength and steadiness when it felt as if my world was falling apart.

Looking back, I'm very proud of those who stuck with the church through the tedious process of rebuilding. Together we were reminded that life is like a pilgrimage, or like a refining process that passes us all through the fire. The question is, what will we be like when we come out on the other side?

COMPANIONS IN THE FIRE

Now fire in the natural, physical sense can accomplish one of two functions: it can destroy, or it can refine, as in the process by which impurities are burned out of gold ore. What results from the smelting process is a precious metal. It is also true that the heat we experience in life can destroy or refine each of us. Tough times can shape a person into a cynic or a saint, into a person who is full of bitterness or fortified with the kind of grace that transcends.

Many today *have* become cynics. To these unhappy folks, life is gloomy and the worst is sure to happen every time and all the time. To them, God is silent, distant, or nonexistent. There are others, even some Christians, for whom life is a perpetual joyride. All is sunshine and God is ready-at-hand with a quick fix-it solution for every problem. That would certainly be nice.

But for the rest of us who, I suspect, make up the majority, life is simply puzzling. We scrape elbows every day with other people who, like us, are imperfect. Occasionally, tragic circumstances or suffering leave us reeling. We believe that God is real—we just have a hard time knowing how to handle the doubts, confusion, and testings of both faith and flesh.

One thing that has strengthened me in tough times is the companionship of others who have felt the fire, too. I've found that companionship among the men and women who have taught me so much about life and faith in my years as a pastor. To me, they are among the everyday heroes, and for that reason their experiences put flesh on these pages. I've also found companionship in the lives of the Bible's great saints—those men and women who found extraordinary strength to face overwhelming odds.

Tough times can shape a person into a cynic or a saint, into a person who is full of bitterness, or one who is fortified with the kind of grace that transcends.

In fact, during my own time of testing I found comfort and insight in the story of three men, Shadrach, Meshach, and Abednego. These Hebrews went through the most famous "fiery trial" of all time. Reading it this time, I gained an understanding I'd never had before.

Many of us cut our teeth on this famous story, found in chapter 3 of the book of Daniel. We heard it at home on our mother's knee, then at Sunday school. It's become so familiar that for many it has lost its power. As adults, we need to reexamine this story in the harsh light of a real and difficult world and ask of it some harder questions.

It is the time of Daniel the prophet. We find God's people in Babylonian captivity sometime between the year 597 B.C., when Nebuchadnezzar destroyed Jerusalem, and 538, when Cyrus the Persian liberated the Hebrews.

Imagine the scene: we are standing on the plains of Dura, outside the palace of the mighty Nebuchadnezzar. Three Hebrew men—Meshach, Shadrach, and Abednego—have risen to positions of prominence. On this day, they are summoned to stand on a platform overlooking the crowds of commoners, amid the king's royal officials. A golden figure, perhaps that of Nebuchadnezzar himself, is carried out by the artisans. The figure is set on a raised altar. The three Hebrew men are facing a moment of truth.

The chief musician lifts his hand, then brings it down to the sound of music— "all kinds of music," the Bible says—from lyres, horns, pipes, cymbals, and the like. At this signal, all the multitudes across this great plain fall to their faces. Likewise, all the toadies of the king's court fall down, trying to show who could grovel the most.

Then one of these toadies looks up. To his shock—and perhaps to his delight—he sees that Meshach, Shadrach, and Abednego are still standing.

Quickly, the three are dragged before Nebuchadnezzar and the charges leveled. The Bible says that the king's face was distorted with rage. He threatens to burn them alive in a furnace. Undoubtedly, the men were beginning to feel a little hot around the collar; I would have.

Quietly, without arrogance, one of them says, "We have no need, O king, to defend ourselves to you. We will not bow to an idol. Whether or not you cast us into a fiery furnace is your affair. Our God is able to deliver us. But even if He doesn't, that's all right too. We'll still trust in Him."

That made Nebuchadnezzar extremely angry. Thinking himself all-powerful, worshiped by thousands upon thousands, he hurls the challenge: "If you refuse to bow, then who is the god who can save you?"

Quite likely, you can recite the rest of the story in your sleep. The music plays again. The three Hebrews will not bow. The furnace is heated "seven times hotter" than normal, and the three men are lifted and carried to it. So hot is that blaze that the guards who throw them in are consumed.

And then the amazing thing happens! An angel of the Lord appears. Their ropes are consumed in flames, but not a hair of their heads is singed. Nebuchadnezzar, realizing he's blown it big, has them taken from the fire. Their clothes do not even smell of smoke.

SOME HARD QUESTIONS

That ends it for most of us. We feel a certain distance between us and these otherworldly events that happened in days gone by. But before we allow the issues to get too clouded, let's ask some very hard questions one at a time.

Immediately, I wonder, "Why do these innocent men—or any good people—have to face trials at all?" It's a reasonable question, and one that God, through this story in Daniel, has no problem addressing.

The first thing I can hear him saying in response is, "Heat is inevitable."

Maybe right at this moment you're facing difficult circumstances. Maybe it's a problem of relationships—irritations at home or on the job. Maybe you feel overwhelmed by moral temptations that strew themselves in your path.

God is not surprised at your difficulties. Jesus said that in this world you will have tribulation. A statement of fact. He did not acknowledge the sunshine patriots who always have everything going their way. Nor did he make this statement with pessimism, but with the purest realism.

There *will* come a day when the world has been fully set to rights. The lion shall lie down with the lamb, our moral battles will be won, and everything will be as it ought.

But that day is not now. And if we go around expecting harmony and justice without struggle, we will be brutally disappointed over and over again. People who hold such high expectations of the world actually allow the world to rule over their emotions, and that is too dangerous in these present, imperfect conditions.

There is a second question I find myself asking: when we're trying to do the right thing, to be good, decent folks, why do some people set out to block or harm us, or seem *intentionally* to misunderstand our motives?

From experience, I have learned something about trying to be a person of integrity. Whenever and wherever there are people trying to live according to principle, to have convictions concerning body or soul, there are also powerful people commanding them to bow down and worship an image other than their God. The world could not tolerate people of principle in the days of Shadrach, Meshach, and Abednego, and the passage of some 2,500 years has not changed things a bit.

Another truth suggests itself to us out of that Babylonian furnace: there are people who want to write your agenda for you—those who will say, "Do it this way or you are wrong."

We can take the pressure off ourselves right from the start by doing what we know is right, even if it drives someone else looney!

GROWING INTO FAITH

Now there is an entirely different aspect of the story of those three Hebrews, something that distances it from most of us. Threatened with death, the three men responded beautifully. They even made an allowance for divine silence in case God didn't intervene. In that attitude, they were cast into the flames—and an angel stepped into the fire to save them.

"Of course," you may say. "Look at the saintly way those men responded. It's no wonder God sent a search-and-rescue party. They were perfect!" Yes, their response *was* remarkable. But I must ask: were they always that way? Did they always respond correctly even in the beginning days of their relationship with God?

You see, many of us mistakenly believe that some people are born saints—and then there's the rest of us, milling about in the mob of humanity. The problem with the saints who walk among us is that they're so *saintly*. It's impossible to identify with them, because they always seem to come through with flying colors.

But I have to wonder if these three Hebrews were born saints, or if they grew into their faith. More than likely, they were veterans. We can do ourselves a favor by taking a long, hard, realistic look at some of the other characters whose lives decorate the pages of Scripture. Think about Abraham, who was a "veteran," handing over Sarah to Pharaoh, lying and saying that she was his sister not his wife in order to save his own skin. And what about David? He wasn't always "a man after God's own heart." He committed adultery, then tried to cover up his sin by committing murder.

We don't always respond as we ought to when the heat is on. Only in my dreams am I Johnny-on-the-spot, making the right decision. Only in hindsight is my vision 20-20. In reality, I often see what I'm *supposed* to do—then I go ahead and bow to the king anyway.

I remember going to a hospital once as a patient, suffering with a kidney stone. The hospital happened to be full, because we lived in a little town that was then experiencing a flu epidemic. I was fortunate in that the head nurse was a member of our church and she managed to get me a private room—fortunate, I say, because I was having no luck passing that stone and was in agony.

I was enjoying my suffering in silence, at least, when in the middle of the night she came to my doorway. She was framed in the light from the hall, and she said, "Pastor, every room in the hospital has two people in it except yours. We have an old man with pneumonia who needs a place. Would it be all right with you to move your bed over to one side and to put him in here?"

I could see the old man's bed outside the door and with him a large entourage of family waiting to come in. My reaction came quick as a flash. "Don't you have some other place to put him?"

Three seconds after, I wished I could have taken those words back. I still live with the disappointed look on the nurse's face.

I have replayed that story many times. Every time I fantasize about it, it has a different ending. I don't make a harsh response at all. I always say something like, "Sure. Bring him on in and I'll be glad to give him my room. Just give me a straight chair out in the hall and let me lean up against a wall. Put a blanket over me and give me an aspirin once in a while. I'll be just fine."

But it didn't play that way in real life.

So I must ask, on behalf of those of us who would have gone into the fire kicking, does God forsake me when I don't respond well to crisis? Is God's presence with me contingent upon my performance? I know there are many who wrestle with that question.

Not long ago, I found myself face to face with a young woman who was laboring under a weight of grief, shame, and remorse.

Church had just ended one Sunday evening and, as I was saying goodnight to folks, this young person, probably in her late twenties, approached me. Her eyes looked sad, hollow. As she shook my hand, I learned her name and that her husband had been an ordained Methodist minister. She asked whether or not I might remember her husband. Something told me I ought to, but I did not. Out came a tragic story.

She had always marveled at her husband's complete dedication to Christ. "A year ago," she told me, "we were driving along a highway when we were involved in a freak accident. My husband was killed instantly.

"I railed against God," she said, her face red with embarrassment. "I cursed him. For a long time, all I've been able to ask is, 'How could you allow that to happen to someone who loved you so much?'"

I was speechless in the face of such deep suffering. Feebly, I tried to come up with a satisfying answer. Before I could speak, her eyes searched mine, pleading for a different answer. "I came tonight just wondering if— " her voice faltered, "if I could ever get back into his Church and into his graces."

The answer came to me all in an instant, surely from outside myself. Taking both her hands in mine, I heard myself say to that suffering sister, "You may feel that you have to crawl in through the back window when no one's looking—but the door is wide open for you. You may have thought you left his graces, but he never left you."

We sometimes put unreasonable expectations on ourselves and then lacerate ourselves when we don't come up to those high standards. But God has us in perspective. He knows we aren't perfect. You and I are a mixture. We are hybrids. It's too late for us to claim innocence. He knows our frame; we are but dust. And because he knows, he understands when we stumble and fall short of even our own expectations.

Like the young woman who had lost her husband, most of us feel we cannot expect God to walk near us when we struggle with pain, loss, or difficulties. We think he will only come to our aid when we have become "perfect." But you cannot clean up the sand in Gethsemane. There was blood on that ground—because God wanted one thing for Jesus, and Jesus wanted something else. He, too, struggled in the heat of the fire.

Shortly after I met the grieving young person, I came in touch with a couple who had also faced heartbreak. This man and woman had been the happy parents of a rambunctious eight-year-old son. Reminiscing, they told me their son was so full of himself he practically turned somersaults up the aisle of the church to hear the children's sermon. Then one day, the boy woke up with blurred vision. A few days later, he couldn't walk right. A malignant brain tumor was found.

A few months later, they buried their son.

As they shared their sorrow with me, I was dumbstruck. When I found my voice, I asked, "What has changed most about you as a result of this experience?"

His eyes shining, the husband squeezed his wife's shoulder and looked at me. "We aren't afraid of the little things anymore," he replied.

That simple but penetrating answer has stuck with me. When you face a hurt you think you can't live through—but you do survive—somehow pain doesn't intimidate you anymore. Yes, you can stand a little heat when you've been through the fire.

To paraphrase the psalmist: "Oh Lord, you tested us and tried us as silver. We've walked through the fire and through deep water. You, oh Lord, have brought us forth into a spacious place" (Psalm 66:10-12).

The prophet Isaiah reaffirmed that promise to us from the Lord, saying, "When you pass through the waters I will be with you . . . when you walk through fire you shall not be burned" (43:2).

Do you feel the heat in some area of your life? Do you lack guidance and direction? Do you feel empty, depressed? Do you need wisdom in handling strained relationships? Do you feel you need more faith? Questions and hurts are not a sign of weakness, they are only the beginning of spiritual growth.

God can take the difficulties of life and, if we enter into the process with him, he will reshape us from the inside out.

The assurance we have from Romans 8 is that God can take the difficulties of life and, if we enter into the process with him, he will reshape us from the inside out. Working together with him, you can create a stronger new you, refashioning doubt into enduring faith, confusion into hope, suffering into joy that overcomes, and weakness into durable strength.

And we will learn a more precious truth: in the white-hot heat of trial, when it feels as though our metal will be consumed, we find at our side an incomparable Friend whose love for us has no end.

How do we begin? A lump of gold ore will always remain a lump of gold ore until it finds itself in skilled hands. In our case, we can *place* ourselves in those hands—the hands of God. Together, working *with* him, we can go about the marvelous work of reshaping our lives into his shining image. Like an apprentice to a goldsmith, our part is to get into a right relationship with him.

That, as we are about to see, is where the process of shaping a new you begins.

2. The Right Path

Experiencing the Transforming Power of God's Love

Life, it has been said, is like a journey down a winding road. Along the way there are many, many crossroads and unexpected turns. At each one, we're faced with questions: should I turn back—or go ahead? Play it safe or risk? There are those who refuse to bother with these troubling questions. Instead they shoulder their pack and forge ahead, with a come-what-may attitude, at least on the surface.

I've met many people for whom life has lost its luster. They meander through the days, lost in their own superficial pursuits. Others have stopped along the road, bemired in a satisfaction with past accomplishments. When they allow themselves to feel at all, however, they sense an emptiness. Some are fearful of change. They creep ahead at a timid pace, unsure, frightened of choices and changes.

Many of these good folks find themselves, sooner or later, at a crossroads. They find that something in their spirit has not been nurtured. They feel dry on the inside. They may even be "good church people," or they may never have warmed a pew. The question underneath is, "What's the meaning in all of this? What am I here for?"

Whether we are aware of it or not, those questions are like the first flames of the refining fire. Their purpose is to make us dissatisfied with the path we are on and the plans we have made on our own. As we become more disquieted, we may lift our eyes for the first time and begin to search for a dimension of life that is deeper.

MY PERSONAL CROSSROADS

I faced disquieting questions myself, as a young man of seventeen. My crossroads happened on a crisp fall evening, beneath a Georgia full moon.

I had stepped outside on the front porch of our small farmhouse to be alone. Inside, mother had cleaned up the supper dishes and gone to her room to be alone. Dad was reading the newspaper. On the cool night wind, I heard a dog's mournful barking. Isolated out there, down an unpaved road thirteen miles from the nearest town where I went to high school, I felt a weight of loneliness.

I sat on the cement step and tried to make sense of the nameless inner longing that had been growing for weeks. I stared at the moonlit row of pines across the road. What I was feeling made no sense. In almost every way, I was headed for good things. Mentally, I made a list.

I faced disquieting questions myself, as a young man of seventeen. My crossroads happened on a crisp fall evening, beneath a Georgia full moon.

I was a senior whose star was on the rise. I had very good grades and was a starter on a winning football team. Thanks to a generous dad, I had money in my pocket and a car at my disposal. Moreover, I had a great group of friends and was dating a pretty brunette named Jean. But even as my list grew, so did the gnawing emptiness. None of these things fully satisfied me. It didn't seem *fair*.

I realized that word—fair—was in some way a challenge flung at God. All my life I'd filled a seat in Sunday school and warmed a pew. Now, as president of the Methodist Youth Fellowship in a church of less than 100, I'd built the group from a handful to more than sixty in a few weeks' time. I'd become president of our MYF subdistrict. Didn't I have a right to feel satisfied?

As I sat there in the dark, the door behind me opened. I heard footsteps, then felt a hand on my shoulder. Mother sat beside me. Gently she asked, "What's wrong, son?"

"Everything's wrong, Mother," I replied, surprised at the intensity of my feelings. "Everything in the world's wrong!"

She sat at my side, her arms around me. The thought that came was frightening: *if life can't be better for me than it is tonight, I don't want to live anymore.* I longed for—what was it?

Quietly, Mother said, "Don't you think it's time you talked to God about it?" Only that; then she stood and went inside.

When I was alone again, my thoughts raced. I realized that, when I'd felt I was on top of the world, my attitude toward God had been, *Show me your best stuff, God, and I'll decide whether or not I'm buying.*

Tonight, however, because I was at the bottom, I prayed, *I'm through with doing it my way. Please show me how you want me to spend the rest of my life. Guide me.*

After a time I went inside.

What happened a little later, as I lay awake in bed, was life-changing. It happened not because I was some special saint, but because God is a good Father who always listens when his children cry out to him. It was as real as the flesh and blood cells that make up my hand—and in its own way just as miraculous.

In the half-light of the full moon through my window, I saw Christ. I have played the scene over and over in my head and it always comes out the same. It was not a dream, yet he was not physically there. I knew suddenly, beyond doubt, his purpose for me was to preach the good news of the gospel. But I had wanted to study law—to shape my life the way I wanted it to be. More than that, my *father* wanted me to study law. Now I had to choose.

An amazing thing occurred the moment I whispered, "I choose *your* way, Lord." Peace rushed over me and filled me. That decision would be tested. There was fire ahead, though I did not know it then. But that night I sealed a pact with God.

TAKING GOD'S PATH

Since I chose to walk God's way that night, I've understood that you cannot go halfway with God. Many of us want to go fifty-fifty with God. More often than that, we want to give less; and then, when we are in a crisis, we expect far more of God. Those crises are not hard to find these days.

Many have observed that we twentieth-century folk seem adrift in our own lives. We move like rootless wanderers from job to job and city to city. We slip out of one marriage and into another. We acquire better homes, faster cars, and more computerized gadgets in a headlong search for happiness. Yet happiness eludes.

How quickly Christians cite "materialism" as the root problem of all our ills. Yet good church people are often ensnared by a creeping sense of lostness. We all fight the loss of hope, the fear of aimless wandering. Gifted pastors as well as gifted business-people become discouraged. Sickness overwhelms. Finances bottom out. Husbands, wives, sons, and daughters fall prey to addictions. Jesus, who told us to be careful of judgments, also said that the rain falls on the just and the unjust (see Matthew 5:45).

The first problem, as I see it, is that some of us never get on the right path in the first place. Several indicators tell us if we are headed in the wrong direction.

When our love for *things* overrides our love for people, we are headed in a wrong direction. When we make power, prestige, status symbols, or a seat atop the corporate ladder our life's goal, we are in deep trouble.

Many, like myself, stumble unexpectedly over our own lostness and wandering. Then we find ourselves asking, "Why? Why was I ever born? Is this all life was meant to be?"

Unfortunately, too many have simply let their souls go to sleep. There are always those who subscribe to the philosophy, "Eat, drink, and be merry, for tomorrow we may die." They live from payday to payday, amusing themselves with expensive "adult toys" on their time off. But for those who have not fallen into this kind of spiritual death, the insistent question will not go away: why *were* you born?

It is all right to ask about the "why" of our existence. But while we're asking, we have to look to the right source for our answers. I had the blessing of a godly mother who helped me remember that "why" is a profoundly religious question, concerning ultimate issues. When we ask "why," we are going back to the beginning—to what happened in the garden, and back to God.

Controversies have swirled around the Genesis story. What really happened? Who made it happen?

I love the yarn about the country preacher who so eloquently retold the creation story for his parishioners, using homey, colorful descriptions. God made Adam out of mud, he told his enrapt listeners, and then leaned him up against a rail fence to dry. "But preacher," a local farmer objected, "if Adam was the first man, where did the rail fence come from?" The preacher replied icily, "It's questions like that that just ruin religion."

And we in the twentieth century have been "ruining" religion much of the time. At crucial points, we insist on absolute clarity when it comes to facts that are unknowable. It is *always* a leap of faith to look back at our common origin and agree, "In the beginning, God . . ."

But when we voice those words, we are immediately confronted with our origin at the hands of a *purposeful* God. We come face to face with one of the major crossroads of our day: either man is a biological accident or else a beloved creation. I must affirm the truth: man is not a biological accident.

When you came into this world, it was because your parents cooperated with God in the creative process. If you want to get in touch with who you are and begin to glimpse where you are headed, start by reading Psalm 139 (verses 13, 14, and 16):

> For thou didst form my inward parts,
>   thou didst knit me together in my mother's womb.
> I praise thee, for thou art fearful and wonderful.
>   Wonderful are thy works! . . .
> Thy eyes beheld my unformed substance;

> in thy book were written, every one of them,
> the days that were formed for me,
> when as yet there was none of them.

Therefore, since we were created, life does not belong to *us*, but to the One who made us. When we choose to become sons and daughters of the Most High God, we know that life belongs to him, and we have solved the riddle of why we were born. We have put our foot forward on the right path.

You see, too many of us have forgotten that life is lived from the *inside*. On our way to achieving the outward signs of success, we've forgotten or neglected the spirit. We are like the prodigal son, who fed one part of his being and starved another. That's why we wind up in the pigpen of life. We are not just a body, we are spirit as well. By choosing to take God's path, no matter what your age or station in life, you can begin to live again on the inside.

IN THE IMAGE OF CHRIST

The Apostle Paul told us that when we place our lives in God's hands we will begin to conform to the image of Christ (see Romans 8:28–30). Whatever does he mean?

To become "like Christ" is to grow in our spiritual resemblance of him much the way a boy grows up with his dad's brow or broad shoulders, or a girl inherits her mother's roses-and-honey complexion. In a spiritual sense, God intends for us to become "look-alikes" with our brother, Jesus Christ.

Immediately, we must also face the fact that there is no other way to grow in inner strength and faith than to be tested. In fact, we will become something less than human if we allow the tough circumstances of life to plow us over, forgetting to ask God what aspect of godly character the smith's hammer and the flame of each affliction is meant to fashion in us. Didn't Simon Peter say, "Beloved, do not be surprised at the fiery ordeal which comes upon you to prove you, as though something strange were happening to you" (1 Peter 4:12).

Our Lord confessed, in face of his trial,

"Now is my soul troubled. And what shall I say?
'Father, save me from this hour'? No, for this
purpose I have come to this hour. Father,
glorify thy name."

(John 12:27–28)

And having suffered the cross for us all, he has now given to each
of us who believe in his name "power to become children of God"
(John 1:12).

That means power in the midst of fear, irritability, uncertainty,
depression, tension, doubt, disappointment. These are the everyday jogs and pitfalls that threaten to pitch us headlong into the
mud. Jesus faced each one of these pitfalls, and it is to him we
must look again and again, daily. How did he handle each trial?
What secret did he learn in facing each one? How can I, like
Jesus, overcome? Because he is our great example, it is to him we
will look throughout the pages of this book.

The Apostle Paul, who knew the secret of the life that overcomes, wrote to encourage us:

One thing I do, forgetting what lies behind
and straining forward to what lies ahead, I press on
toward the goal for the prize of the upward call of God
in Christ Jesus.

(Philippians 3:13–14)

We are beckoned by God, and his power draws us on. We do
not have to be mired by emotions or painful circumstances.

Are you dissatisfied with some aspect of your life? Are you
facing struggles big or small? The first step is up to you. As you
take the leap of faith, reaching out to God, you will find One
waiting who will never leave or forsake you. He will stick closer
than a brother; he has promised to see you all the way through.

He created you. Will you entrust your life into his capable
hands?

He alone can lead you from the emptiness that lies in every human spirit. And he will, if you will ask him. Then, together, you can move toward the next step, which is conformity to his eternal purpose and goal for you.

The first step is up to you. As you take the leap of faith, reaching out to God, you will find One waiting who will never leave or forsake you.

---

3. A Matter of Focus
Living with a Purpose

One symptom of today's rampant search for meaning, oddly enough, is our unprecedented scramble for personal happiness. It's odd, I say, because there has never been so much time, energy, and money spent by so many who want to be happy but are not. Ask any therapist or pastoral counselor. Everyone from the vacation industry to the medical community is getting into the act with false remedies for the unhappiness that plagues our age.

A conservative estimate by one of the news magazines has put the cost of our "happiness" in excess of $50 billion a year. That's how much Americans spend going to far-off places, buying expensive recreational "toys" and gadgets, not to mention the time and energy spent. We spend additional billions buying stuff to swallow. Just the other day, I heard about a new tranquilizer that's supposed to be especially effective. It doesn't help you relax, but it makes you feel good about being tense.

You would hope that we are learning some things along the way. For instance, that *pleasure* is not the same as happiness: pleasure is short-lived; that which brings us pleasure today can later bring boredom, even despair. True happiness, that elusive, intangible substance, is so hard to define. But perhaps we are beginning to see that happiness cannot be bought, drunk, eaten, worn, traveled to, or swallowed in a capsule. It doesn't come from sky-diving, vacationing in Cancun, or dining at chic restaurants.

How do you find true happiness?

Could it be that Aldous Huxley, the famed British author, was right when he said that everybody strains after happiness and the result is, no one is happy?

In one respect, I believe Huxley's statement is accurate. The most miserable people in the world are those whose highest goal is their own satisfaction. Such people drive themselves, becoming almost manic in their search for happiness, no matter what the cost to their spouse or children, no matter what the collective cost to their family or friends. For such people, there is no contentment, and usually only remorse for the years wasted and the hearts broken on the way.

However, I disagree with Huxley when he says that "no one is happy." We would be in a sorry state if an unbelieving humanist were allowed to pass the final judgment on the spiritual well-being of humankind.

We are beginning to see that happiness cannot be bought, drunk, eaten, worn, traveled to, or swallowed in a capsule. It doesn't come from sky-diving, vacationing in Cancun, or dining at chic restaurants.

Still, what is true about Huxley's observation is this: happiness never yields its joys to those who seek it *directly*.

Picture in your mind a Christmas card that was sent to me—it was one of those optical illusion cards that always give me so much trouble! When you first look at it, you see an artistic rendering of a towering, snow-covered mountain, the shadows of pine trees and rocky crevasses lining its slopes—a pristine, winter scene. But if you move your eyes just slightly, catching the mountain scene in your peripheral vision, you see hidden in its shadings the face of Jesus. Stare at it directly, and it's a mountain again; glance aside, and see the face of the Savior.

In a similar way, you can go out with clenched fists and taut jaw, saying, "I'm going to find happiness, no matter what." You'll never find it. Finding happiness, like seeing the face of Jesus on the card, is something we come to only *in*directly.

Or, conversely, happiness is all a matter of what we focus on. Robert Orbin, in *Quote Magazine*, said, "Whether or not we live happily ever after is determined in large part by what we're after."

A HEART CENTERED ON GOD

Let me ask you directly: what is your heart centered on?

If we are self-centered, absorbed only with fulfilling our own ego needs, we quickly come to dislike the self we have shaped. Strangely, the person who sees his or her own dreams destroyed is sometimes the one who finds a greater treasure.

Susan is such a person.

A beautiful young woman with auburn hair, Susan was an athletic teenager who especially enjoyed water sports. Since her father owned a boat company, many a summer afternoon would find Susan skiing behind one of the finest and fastest outboards on the water. But tragedy was waiting.

One day, Susan was riding in a car with her brother John. She was chipper, full of life. In fact, it was her sixteenth birthday. Before she knew what was happening, there was a screeching of brakes, the twisting of metal—then she was knocked unconscious.

When Susan half-woke, in a daze of pain, bright lights burned her eyes. The crisp white sheets, the intravenous needle, and the smell of antiseptic told her she was in a hospital emergency room. She had no idea where John was. She tried to shift. Her legs would not move. Weak with pain, she shut her eyes.

As consciousness grew, she became aware of a conversation in the corridor just outside her room. To her shock and horror, she overheard a doctor telling her father, "Your daughter's legs are paralyzed." Then she heard her father's sobs.

Some moments later, her father and the doctor came into the room and stood beside the bed. Her father's face, so pale, so downcast, said it all as he silently took her hand.

The doctor, finding the words her father could not, said plainly, "Honey, you will never be able to walk again."

But in those few bleak minutes before they'd come in, Susan had prayed. A remarkable calm lifted her. Because she had a personal faith in God, she had no doubt that it came from outside of herself. Looking her doctor in the eye, she blurted, "But I can still use my hands."

From that moment, Susan began on the upward trail. To be sure, there were trying times ahead—a long hospital stay, the knowledge that her brother's head injury would leave him permanently impaired, not to mention the daily reality of life in a wheelchair. But each morning, she determined to fix her eyes on things other than her personal tragedy. She had begun, with her hand in God's, to let her life be reshaped from the inside.

Some steps in Susan's growth were small. The first thing she did was to ask for her crochet hook. Her grandmother had taught her the skill. Even before Susan was released from the hospital a steady stream of crocheted gifts for friends and family flew from her hands.

Other steps were much larger, more challenging, and more painful. As soon as she was able, Susan returned to her high school, day by day wheeling herself past the gymnasium where she'd once excelled among her peers. Her faith and determination astonished and inspired her parents through the heartbreak of their double tragedy. She finished with grades high enough to allow her to attend Rice University, a school reserved for those with solid academic ability, where she earned a degree in accounting.

Only recently did I meet Susan, who related this story to me. And I must tell you just a few of the other wonderful things about her. After college, she continued to enter into life's challenges and creative process, hand-in-hand with her Creator. She met and married a man who now works with her father in the boating business, and subsequent years brought them three children. Today, Susan is an active wife, mother, and a CPA. Her radiance is an inspiration, a joy and comfort to all who know her.

There is a stirring lesson for each of us in Susan's personal victory. If we focus on the obstacles in our path, on limitations, or if we give in to self-pity, we chain ourselves to misery. But if we set our eyes on something *useful*, something greater than ourselves, we will be remade by an inner joy. And one day we will awaken to the fact that contentment has come. Happiness is a by-product of helping God in his projects and purposes and in the daily running of our ordinary world.

GOD HAS A PURPOSE FOR EACH OF US

There are so many who chafe against the fact that they cannot be physically or visibly active. I know so many mothers who are at home with small children, so many elderly, so many confined by illness. And there are even healthy, able young people who feel they are of little use to God because they cannot teach Sunday school or wave a Bible from a pulpit. Often, one of these people comes to me with a long face and says, "I'm not much use."

I heartily disagree—not because I'm trying to salve and numb empty hearts. Rather, I *know* that God has a purpose, a useful ministry for each of us.

Bishop Arthur Moore of the Methodist Church loved to tell about an experience he had in the days of the old steam locomotive.

If we set our eyes on something useful, something greater than ourselves, we will be remade by an inner joy.

Riding through the south one time, in those bygone days, Moore's train stopped periodically to take on coal and water. In one backwater town, when the train pulled up to a siding, Moore opened his window and leaned out to get a breath of fresh air. Against the side of the depot, half-dozing in the summer sun, was an old man.

Hailing him, Moore said, "Tell me something, sir. Do the people in this town enjoy their religion?"

Quick as a flash, the old man replied, "Them that has it do."

Yes, Christianity *is* a joyous faith. When we get into it, and it gets into us, and reshapes us, we start to move beyond a preoccupation with our problems and focus on binding up the wounds of others. Then the marvelous thing begins to happen: we discover a quality of usefulness, be it in prayer or in quiet, simple service, that turns a gray existence into a constant brightness.

I know several remarkably happy people. I say their happiness is remarkable, because the outward circumstances confronting each of these good folks could easily make anyone unhappy.

I think of John Paul Hodanbosi, whose love and faithfulness move me whenever I see him seated in our church here in Houston. He is a man of modest means and is now in his eighties, but that did not deter him for a moment when he heard about the needs of the many hungry people in our city—for many of them were his neighbors. While most were feeling helpless in the face of such need, Mr. Hodanbosi found a way to respond to the crisis.

The first thing he did was secure from a local grocery store a beat-up cart—one of those with a front wheel that wobbles furiously when it's pushed. Making his way along the sidewalks, he then went through his neighborhood, visiting all the grocery stores within walking distance. At each one, the manager agreed to give him the fruit, bread, and other staples that were no longer fresh enough to be in their display cases.

So began a service of love. Each day, whether in summer or winter, Mr. Hodanbosi pushes his grocery cart with the wobbling wheel down to the grocery stores. When it's fully loaded, he pushes it through the poor neighborhoods where every piece of fruit, every loaf of bread is gratefully received.

Perhaps you're not the kind of person who finds it easy to go out onto unknown streets like John Paul Hodanbosi. That need not stop you. There is no place in more need of your help, no place more able to equip you for good service, than your local church.

When it comes to serving the church, I am reminded of a Mrs. Durden, an elderly woman in poor health who was a member of the first church I served. At that time, there were only sixty-nine members, and we were trying to build a sanctuary.

This woman had very little in terms of this world's goods, but she had a tremendous desire to help. She said to me, "I can't make a financial pledge, but I can bake cakes." I had no idea what she meant. Later, I learned.

In part, she made her living by baking cakes for people in the community. She did not drive or get out much, so they would bring the ingredients to her. And when they learned about her desire to contribute to the church, they began to bring her extra ingredients—a few more eggs, a little more flour. Then Mrs. Durden could bake more cakes, which her little grandson would take to the corner drugstore to be sold.

Few gifts moved me more than when Mrs. Durden gave the proceeds from her cake sales to help build that new sanctuary. She gave what she had—or rather, she gave it all she had.

PRAYER: THE HIGHEST MINISTRY

And then there are those who say to me, "I can't even bake. Why, I don't do anything right. All I can do is pray."

Pray? That's all you can do? How I long for every one of those good folks to know that the highest ministry of all is intercessory prayer! I wish I could introduce everyone who feels useless to a woman I knew. Her name was Eva Crawley.

Eva lived in a tiny trailer with a wooden ramp leading to its door. The ramp had served a purpose in the days when Eva could be moved in a wheelchair. In her last years, however, she was confined to bed, her body horribly twisted and distorted with arthritis. Her son, a chicken farmer who lived next door, assisted his mother in between gathering and washing eggs.

The first time I entered her trailer, sympathy was showing on my face.

"Big boy," she said, "don't feel sorry for me! There are lots of things I can do. If someone will turn the pages, I can read. And if my son hands me a wet cloth and lays some eggs beside me, I can help him by washing eggs. I'm a good egg washer. Some days I can wash more than a dozen."

During the months that followed, I regularly visited that cheerful, courageous woman. I discovered that many people came to see her. She had cultivated a grace and gratitude about the small

CHRIST UNITED METHODIST CHURCH
4488 POPLAR AVENUE
MEMPHIS, TENNESSEE 38117

things, and I suspect that made us happier with our lot in life. And we knew she prayed for each one of us.

It was what I learned about Eva Crawley after her death that surprised me.

Several years after I'd been called to serve in another church, I received the message late one night that she had passed away. Having promised her on our last visit that I would have a part in her funeral, I got up early the next day to make the drive.

As I approached the church, however, I could find no place to park anywhere near it! Although it was a half hour before the funeral, people were already having to park along the road and walk the rest of the way through the sandy ruts.

As I approached, I saw that the church itself was already full and a crowd had formed on the grass lawn outside. Some men were stringing up loudspeakers in the trees so everyone could hear the service.

Many people spoke to me that day. I learned that in the crowd were four men who gave Eva Crawley credit for their being in the ministry. There were countless ones whom she had consoled and cheered—hundreds of us for whom she had prayed. All the time I kept hearing a bright voice from the past saying, "I can wash eggs . . ." And I heard another voice saying, "Well done!"

People like Eva Crawley have caused me to see the great usefulness in prayer, an occupation that may seem senseless in our world with its emphasis on activity.

In fact, because of what these "prayer warriors" have taught me, there are prayer boxes all over the sanctuary of First Methodist Church. At each service, prayer requests from our members are placed inside. When a request is received, our thirty-six prayer captains go into action. They notify each other of the need by phone, then each one notifies his or her team members. Within hours, thirty-six prayer teams are on their knees!

FOCUSING ON GOD'S PLANS

What is the connection between folks like John Paul Hodanbosi, Mrs. Durden, Eva Crawley, and all who work at the occupation of prayer? What makes people like Susan able to go on, even when many of life's joys are torn from them in a crippling accident?

They have learned that the victory on the inner journey is all a matter of what you set your sights on.

Jesus put it another way. To those who would become his disciples, he said,

> "For whoever would save his life will lose it, and
> whoever loses his life for my sake will find it. . . .
> For the Son of man is to come with his angels in
> the glory of his Father, and then he will repay every
> man for what he has done."
>
> (Matthew 16:25, 27)

Victory on the inner journey is all a matter of what you set your sights on.

Once you begin to set aside your own plans and focus on his plans, you will discover the wellspring of happiness. In the contented person, you find an inner poise, an inner strength even when things go dreadfully wrong. Why is this so?

A friend of mine helped me to understand the attitude of heart that allowed him to live in joy in the midst of every circumstance. He surprised me one day by saying that his favorite statement from the whole Bible is, "And it came to pass . . ."

At first, I couldn't see how he read much of anything into that little phrase. But as he spoke, my eyes were opened to new vistas.

To him, the very fact that all things pass is a great promise. It implies that every dark day will soon be followed by a new dawn; that every crisis will resolve; that this world is temporary, but God is eternal. Not only that, but whatever we do at God's direction will stand forever.

David, who knew the depths of despair and the heights of joy, wrote,

> Happy is he whose help is the God of Jacob,
>   whose hope is in the Lord his God,
> who made heaven and earth,
>   the sea, and all that is in them;
> who keeps faith for ever.
>
>   (Psalm 146:5–6)

Quite likely it was at David's knee that Solomon, the wisest man who ever lived, learned to say,

> Happy is he who trusts in the Lord.
>   (Proverbs 16:20)

The person whose life is grounded in God, who trusts God at his Word, is happy. That person's soul is quiet, knowing that, whatever the outward circumstances, all will be well.

With this unshakable happiness in our hearts, which no earthly pleasure can give, we become like a strong beacon shining in the darkness of this world. We become, in Jesus' words, the light of the world, a city on a hill that cannot be hidden (Matthew 5:14).

A person who focuses on a purpose beyond his or her own need finds usefulness. When we fit into God's plan we find our focus in service, in giving of what we have, and in prayer.

Then we find, in his hands, inner resources to carry us on our way.

4. A New Disposition
From Irritability to Right Relationships

Spirituality is a funny thing. You can drive through scenic mountains, sensing an "all's right with the world" feeling deep in your soul. And a moment later, when another driver cuts you off, you explode with anger. Not a shred is left of that inner peace.

Beginning to let God mold and shape you spiritually, as we discussed in the first three chapters, is one thing. Many, however, find that, after getting their relationship with God right, only one huge obstacle remains—*other people!* As one lady put it, "I could get along just fine if everybody would just do right." But what about when they don't "do right"? Do we give in to all our irritations? Go off and live a hermit's life in a secluded cabin? You'd probably be bothered by hikers!

The poet John Donne observed, "No man is an island." Every time we turn around, it seems, someone is rubbing us the wrong way. Relationships are strained at work, at home. Marriages break up, parents and children become alienated, friends stop talking to one another. One of the signs most characteristic of our time is a universal concern with strained relationships.

Conflicts and broken relationships like these are even a problem among Christians. There is a wry little verse, in fact, that relates:

> To live with all the saints in heaven,
> that will be bliss and glory.
> But to live with the saints here below
> is quite another story.

This is reminiscent of the well-known anecdote about the little girl who prayed, "Dear Lord, help the bad people to be good and help the good people to be nice."

Sometimes we Christians are not especially easy folk to get along with nor do we always know how to resolve conflict.

And yet we know that we are supposed to get along with others, to be peacemakers and create harmony in the world around us. We know that right relationships are fulfilling. A study conducted by the Stanford Research Institute evaluated the personal habits of some of the most successful people in the country. You might expect that the individuals studied would rate diligence or creativity or punctuality as the biggest reason for their success. In fact, researchers learned the following: 12 percent of those polled attributed their success to knowledge and skill; 88 percent attributed success to their ability to get along with other people.

If the Stanford study is even close to accurate, then we can agree with the person who said, "What most people today need is not a new *position*, but a new *disposition*."

WORKING ON STRAINED RELATIONSHIPS

The Apostle Paul, who spent so much time traveling among the first-century churches, was not isolated from the problem of strained relationships. In his letter to the people of Galatia, we find that he knew exactly what they needed in order to correct their poor behavior toward each other—that is, they needed a new disposition.

Twelve percent of those polled attributed their success to knowledge and skill; 88 percent attributed success to their ability to get along with other people.

In the letter, Paul writes, "But if you bite and devour one another take heed that you are not consumed by one another" (Galatians 5:15). Paul was saying, "Beware, or the community of faith will be destroyed."

I note that Paul used the strongest language possible, employing Greek words for "bite and devour" which depict wild animals tearing at each other in a life-and-death battle. He was not writing a theological treatise about the struggle between the spirit and the flesh; he was referring to the Galatians's awful behavior in everyday relationships. In effect, he was saying, "I'm talking about the problem of irritability."

Later, in the same letter to the same irritable people, Paul catalogues the sins of the flesh. There is something interesting about this list. It contains several groupings: sins of fleshly sensuality; sins of heathen idolatry; and sins against the body, such as drunkenness. By far the largest group, however, consists of some eight problems, all having to do with conflicts between people: hatred, discord, jealousy, fits of rage, selfish ambition, dissensions, factions, and envy. If you have any or all of these traits, Paul says, they will keep you continually in conflict with your neighbor.

Now some of us, reading that list, have just gotten a rather uncomfortable reminder that certain relationships we're involved in are not going very well. We can probably all pinpoint the trait—whether selfishness or jealousy or what have you—that caused the two personalities to chafe. And usually, if we think about it, we find that there is at least one sin from Paul's list that crops up over and over in so many of our relationships—let's say it's anger. However, we must often confront a deeper problem.

Many of us spend all our time telling ourselves that anger, for instance, is a habit. We say, "That's just the way I am, and I guess I'll never change." When we think like this, we become lazy in our dealings with other people.

Recently, I boarded a rather crowded airplane and found my assigned seat. A few minutes later, I saw another clergyman coming down the aisle. Everyone could see he was a minister because he wore a clerical collar. The other thing you noticed about him right away was his size. He was immensely overweight, so obese that the aisle was almost not wide enough for him to squeeze through. And leading him, holding his ticket, was a petite flight attendant who apparently was trying to help him find his seat.

Not far from me, the attendant stopped at one row of seats, checked the ticket, then pointed to the middle seat. Evidently, the minister had asked for an aisle seat, because his immediate and loud reaction was to turn the air blue with profanity. He let it fly. Heads turned, eyebrows shot up. As a fellow minister, I didn't know whether to offer him my seat or crawl under it for embarrassment.

It was apparent that this man had spent very little time cultivating self-control. He was a walking billboard that said, "I'm irritated, and I have a right to be. Furthermore, I don't care whom I inflict with my anger!"

So much of what we hear today from secular psychology tells us it's okay to follow our visceral reactions, our fleshly impulses, our glands. But when we do, we inevitably exhibit the sinful traits Paul warns against, and our lives are defined by a host of irritations with other people. Paul is clear, however, that we don't have to be controlled by "the flesh." We have a choice in the matter.

TRAITS OF A NEW DISPOSITION

Through the power of the Holy Spirit, we can be free to rise above all that would ruin our ability to love others truly. The option Paul shows us is not an unhealthy repression of our impulses, it's not programming yourself to say that an irritation doesn't exist, or turning off your feelings and doing violence to your emotional health. Paul tells us, though, that we don't have to be controlled by knee-jerk reactions to the people who rub us the wrong way. We can respond in keeping with the divine nature. A new Christ-like disposition is available to us. We can be reshaped by the power of God's love working in us.

What are the characteristics of that new disposition? They are, Paul says, "the fruit of the Spirit."

Some have observed that the nine attributes listed in Galatians 5:22–23 describe the disposition of Jesus himself. Look at those nine fruits and you will know what Jesus was like: love, joy, peace, patience, kindness, goodness, faithfulness, gentleness, self-control.

Paul said that if you will let yourself be a Spirit-led person rather than following the evil impulses of your flesh, you will demonstrate these attributes in your life. You will begin to show forth the very disposition of Jesus in the world. Then you won't have to worry about finding yourself a good deed to do, or worry about becoming irritable. Because the attitude of Jesus will have worked itself so completely into your soul, manifesting itself in your demeanor, your attitudes, and your whole approach to life, you will do people good just by being around them, by working where they work, by living in the house where they live.

At once, some may say, "That sounds wonderful, but I know how irritable I can get. It's a bad habit with me." How true that is: irritability is a learned behavior, a habit. We don't have to think about it, we just do it—the way we splash water on our face in the morning, or brush our teeth, or comb our hair. But don't let anyone persuade you that a habit can't be modified or changed. If habits are learned, they can be unlearned. In the same way we have cultivated those personal habits, having performed them over and over thousands of times, we can also cultivate a new disposition.

I have specifically used the word cultivate, because in order to make our response habitually Christian, we have to work at it. We are not born with good habits anymore than we are born with good character. And if we don't work at learning Christ-like, Spirit-led responses, then some other kind of response will fill the vacuum.

The exciting news that Paul gives to the Galatians is that we can choose the kind of behavior pattern we want to establish. Choosing is the way we establish our habits, make no mistake. I am telling you that you can, you *must* deliberately choose to be kind in a situation when things aren't going your way. Through the Spirit's empowerment, you can deliberately repeat the pattern of choosing to respond with love, joy, peace, patience, cultivating a new disposition. Repeated regularly enough, sooner or later you will establish a habitual, godly response to any rub.

Are you still objecting? Are you saying, "Most of the time, I react without thinking—I get angry, impatient, snappish before I know what I'm doing"? Then, with God's help, the first step is to take those responses out of the realm of ingrained habit and put them back into your conscious thought processes again.

The first step is simply to pull our behavioral responses up to the front of our minds and examine them. When do I react impatiently? How am I provoked to anger? When am I unkind? Of whom am I jealous? When we perform this examination prayerfully, in the white light of God's divine presence, we invite his dynamic Spirit into the process. He will show us the how, what, when, and why of habitual responses.

Some may say, "I don't have to think about it. I already *know* what bends me out of shape! I even plan to be nice—I really want to be. But then I find myself right smack in the middle of it, frustrated, and the steam-valve lets loose." Someone has said that we have forty-five miles of nerves in our body. Imagine that— forty-five miles! Some days it feels as though we have a hundred miles of nerves and the last sixty of them are exposed, raw. How can we—when we are kept waiting, when we are frustrated or stymied—how can we cultivate the right response, not sitting at home in an armchair thinking about it, but out in the real world at the very moment we are tempted to react badly?

CULTIVATING HEALTHY RESPONSES

I want to tell you about a valuable technique I learned from Dr. W. E. Sangster, the noted British Methodist preacher. I once heard Dr. Sangster say in a sermon that he meditated on the fruits of the Spirit daily. In fact, he had combined them in some way so that he had reduced them to seven, one for each day of the week. In those moments when delay caused him to become frustrated, he would short-circuit irritation by meditating on patience. He did this so often that patience, he suddenly discovered, was no longer a conscious, determined response—it was part of him. He *was* patient.

I must admit, I've thought about Dr. Sangster often, because I experience frustration repeatedly. For one thing, I'm the worst "line picker" in the world. I have not met anyone who can match me for picking the wrong line, whether at a drive-in bank or a walk-in bank, wherever I go. In my family, we call it "Hinson's Law": if there's a wrong line, I'm sure to be in it. You know what I'm talking about, don't you?

One line may stretch out the door, and the other line has only three people. You know which one I choose and you can imagine what happens. The teller or the cashier gets a phone call from Zimbabwe or slides an "out to lunch" sign on the counter right in my face. All the folks in the longer line will finish before I do. I respond as well to that as I do to the news that I need a root canal. You get the picture.

Now I know I'm not alone in this. Some of you are in that wrong line behind me! What happens next is that we fret and fume and run up our blood pressure. The irritation doesn't stop there; we spoil the day at work and when we get home we still have enough frustration to spray all over the family. And unchecked, we can fall into a pattern of making less than our best response to circumstances beyond our control.

Therefore, I did not reduce the nine fruits of the Spirit to seven, as Dr. Sangster did. I left them at nine, because I sometimes need *two* on Mondays and other especially trying occasions. But let me tell you what happened when I began to apply his idea.

The other day, I was driving down the freeway—I was late for an appointment. Not only that, I got stopped in heavy traffic. Now, no one plans for these delays, and I sat there trying to keep cool with the air-conditioner running. All the while though, I was more conscious of my own internal radiator, which was beginning to boil; and I was about to do all sorts of bad things to myself physiologically and emotionally.

Then I remembered: "Hinson, today is Tuesday. Today you're supposed to be meditating about peace."

Inwardly, I groaned. Not peace! Not in this messed-up traffic, with my schedule shot to bits. But it was Tuesday and the word for the day was *peace*. Besides, I knew I needed help.

So I got into it. The first thing that came to mind was the story about Jesus and his disciples crossing the Sea of Galilee when a storm blew up. Jesus was sleeping like a baby on the boat as it rocked on those fierce waves. The disciples shook him and shouted, "Wake up, Lord. We're all going to drown." Jesus stood up then and said to the sea, "Peace. Be still." The winds calmed. The tossing waves became smooth as glass.

Pretty soon, as I reflected on Christ's ability to give peace, I felt a little bit of it come into my own soul. The traffic moved a little, and I thought some more. And a little more peace came. I tell you, by the end of that hectic day, because I'd been reflecting on peace all along, I thought, "Lord, we had a beautiful time out there in traffic, didn't we?" The Lord made that delay into an occasion for growth.

Why? Because at the moment emotion was tearing me apart, I turned it over to the Spirit within. You see, Christ *wants* to fill us with the fruit of his Spirit. He wants us to have his mind in all things. When we reflect on his disposition, when we think about the character traits that describe him, a door opens within. Every single time we meditate on him, he walks through that door into our lives, giving us, little by little and more and more, his character.

When we talk about meditation, however, we have an immediate problem. Most modern Christians have little or no idea how to meditate. There are several nonbiblical types of meditation around today. We need to understand what they are in order to distinguish.

One is Transcendental Meditation, or TM, which comes from the Eastern religions. The idea is to repeat over and over a word or a single syllable that makes no sense to you, until you have blanked out your personality and your mind is completely empty. The idea is to allow the *self* to come into contact with the great "consciousness" of the universe and to feel better about yourself. The danger here is that you come to idolize yourself.

Another type of meditation that is common, especially among entrepreneurs and salespeople, is the technique called "visualizing your goals." For instance, you picture yourself as happy, successful, wearing expensive three-piece suits and driving a late-model car. Some who teach this kind of meditation—for that's really what it is—go so far as to suggest that you cut out pictures of the object of your desire—say, a Mercedes—and post them where you can see them every day. The idea here is to focus your thoughts so greatly on a desired object or goal that all of your energies are bent toward it. The danger here, of course, is that you idolize material possessions.

LEARNING BIBLICAL MEDITATION

What, then, do we mean by biblical meditation? And how is it done? This is the method I have learned, and it may be helpful to you.

First, I set aside time to be alone and have a devotional period. This may seem almost too simple to mention, but the fact is that many Christians do not spend time cultivating spiritual health. We are so hung up on digital time; we are so task-oriented. For many, the idea of taking time to meditate seems a waste. We need to see life in a larger framework; that is, we need to tap into the realm of the eternal, which is not pressured by time.

Then I choose an image from Scripture. Let's say it's that of the storm-tossed sea—a picture that often comes to mind when I know I'm going to be faced with a tumultuous day. I allow my imagination to carry me into the scene: I smell the salt spray and see the dark, cresting waves.

Then I refocus below the rolling waves—twenty-five feet down, one hundred feet down. There, all is undisturbed, peaceful. Gradually, I begin to feel some of that indescribable calm coming into my own life and circumstances.

The Bible indicates that Christ can give us a peace that the world cannot give or take away. I believe the calmness that comes by centering on him never fully leaves us, no matter how tough the schedule nor how difficult the duties. There can remain within us a reservoir of peace, and if we find ourselves in a traffic jam (or the wrong end of a long line!), we can dip into that reservoir and find real rest for our souls.

Another favorite scriptural image is that of Jesus on the Mount of Beatitudes. Because, as a pastor, I come in contact with so many people each day, this image is especially helpful. I imagine Jesus' expression—and especially his eyes—as he looks out across that green hillside with its multitude of faces. As he sees their hurts, their anxieties, their feelings of guilt and unworthiness, an unspeakable compassion lights his eyes.

And later, as I move through my day, I cannot help but feel that same kind of compassion as I am greeted by the hurting, anxious, and troubled men and women whom I encounter.

You see, biblical meditation cannot be contained behind the closed doors of the room where you have your devotions. Because you are reshaping your whole thought process, the renewing strength you find in meditation moves into your active world.

And so the fruit of the Spirit enriches our lives and, through us, the lives of other people. It becomes a bastion of inner peace when we must cope with people-problems, even with those folks who irritate us most.

I must confess that, even though a pastor is supposed to be patient and kind with everyone, there is that rare individual who gets to you every time.

I am reminded of a crisp, February afternoon when I wanted to be out hunting with my bird dogs but was obligated to make some pastoral calls. Even worse, I was scheduled to visit a person who fell into the category of those I call "sour saints with shriveled souls"—a person who whines and complains about everything!

As I turned in at the walk leading to this person's front door, I was feeling quite pious, congratulating myself for doing my duty in this difficult task. Just before I reached the steps, however, I noticed something lying in the grass. A tiny English sparrow lay beside the walk in the frosted grass, its wings frozen in death.

The fruit of the Spirit enriches our lives and, through us, the lives of other people. It becomes a bastion of inner peace when we must cope with people-problems, even with those folks who irritate us most.

Jesus' words leapt at me from Matthew's Gospel (10:29, 31): "Are not two sparrows sold for a penny? And not one of them will fall to the ground without your Father's will . . . Fear not, therefore; you are of more value than many sparrows."

I stood, envisioning the great God of the universe stopping to take note of the death of this tiny bird. With that picture in mind, I straightened my slumping shoulders, feeling much less pious now. I went inside knowing that, whether sweet or sour, God loves each of his children. All through the visit, which was riddled with the usual complaints, I never lost the sense that every single individual is of infinite worth to our heavenly Father.

We are not talking about mind-games. We are talking about learning to see from a new perspective people who rub us the wrong way. Our disposition is always to put people down; God's disposition is to raise them to a new place of value.

Do you want a new disposition? Do you want to make a habitually Christian response to the irritations confronting you?

There is a process involved, make no mistake about it. You cannot expect to change ingrained responses overnight. But you can begin today to develop the fruit of the Spirit in your life. Make that choice. Cultivate the disposition of Jesus Christ. Let it infuse your entire life.

You will be amazed at the transformation that will begin to take place in you from the inside out as you relearn how to relate to other people. This is the divine brightness that Paul referred to as "Christ in you, the hope of glory!"

This glory is available to all who cultivate the life of the Spirit. It is available to you.

5. The Growing Edge

Reshaping Disappointments into Growing Experiences

Recently, I read a book to which all of us could probably contribute a chapter: *The Book of Failures.* In it the author, Stephen Pyle, tells about all kinds of situations in which people have met with drastic disappointment.

For instance, he tells the story of a woman in London whose cat got stuck up in a tall tree. She summoned the fire department to get her precious pet down. In no time, a huge rig pulled up and a firefighter bravely climbed the ladder and rescued the cat. The woman was so grateful that she invited the whole crew in for tea. After the tea and biscuits were gone, the firefighters climbed back in the truck and backed out, forgetting to look behind them. To the woman's utter horror, they backed over the cat.

Who among us has not had some disappointment, funny or not so funny, great or small? Perhaps no disappointment is so great as when other people, and especially those we love the most, let us down.

Jesus experienced great disappointment at the hands of his closest friends. When you look at the biblical record, you find that those men we honor today as the apostles were quite a ragtag lot and not very stable.

In the Gospels, we read about Jesus' miraculous feeding of the five thousand as his twelve hand-picked followers look on in amazement. Not long after that, however, we see those same twelve men traveling together and squabbling among themselves because someone forgot to bring enough food for supper.

The Apostle John, who was among Jesus' closest friends, gives us one of the few clues as to how Jesus was able to avoid disillusionment. He reports simply that Jesus knew what was in the heart of man (John 2:25). In short, he had no illusions!

It is to the Apostle Paul that we turn to enlarge our understanding of the kind of faith that can overcome when hopes are dashed. In 2 Corinthians he describes a series of setbacks that would entirely wipe out most of us. With heart-wrenching honesty, the great apostle confesses that he has been troubled on every side, perplexed, persecuted, and cast down. He lists the harrowing experiences he went through, all for the sake of spreading the gospel, and they make you cringe: beaten with rods, stoned, imprisoned, shipwrecked—and probably worst of all, rejected by most of his own countrymen. Yet he says that he is not distressed, that he is not in despair, nor is he destroyed!

I will be the first to admit that it is hard to imagine so gallant a response to such painful adversity. I can more readily identify with another figure from the Scriptures, who did not handle disappointment well at all.

This man's name was Ahab, and at one time he was king of Israel. I think there is an important lesson to gain by considering this fellow and his experience.

In 1 Kings chapter 21, we find Ahab to be the kind of man who is always grasping. Next to his palace was a beautiful vineyard belonging to a man named Naboth. Though Ahab had great wealth, he wasn't satisfied. He wanted Naboth's vineyard so he could turn it into a little pleasure garden.

Ahab went to Naboth and said, "I must have this land. Let's exchange properties. I'll give you a piece of mine for this parcel." And if that deal wasn't sweet enough, Ahab offered him money instead.

The vineyard, however, had belonged to Naboth's father and his father's father, and it was his obligation to keep it in the family for his sons and grandsons. You must understand that the idea of inheritance was strongly rooted in the Hebrew culture. It was a right of peasants and kings alike, a fact that is spelled out in the Bible. So Naboth had every right to respond as he did, which was to say, "No way. I don't care how much you offer in land or money. You cannot have my family's land."

How did Ahab take this refusal? The Bible tells us he was vexed and sullen. He went back to his palace and crawled in bed, where he turned his face to the wall and would not eat.

Now putting on the sulks gets people's attention, doesn't it? Ahab's wife, the infamous Jezebel, came and asked what was wrong. When Ahab told her, she set in motion a scheme that culminated in the murder of Naboth. Even though it meant shedding the blood of an innocent man, nothing stopped King Ahab from planting a garden for his own disgusting delight.

Obviously, few of us would go that far to satisfy a disappointment. However, most of us become "vexed and sullen" sometimes, don't we? (I never knew my mother was using a biblical word when she used to tell me I was being sullen.) When things don't go our way, we're all tempted to go home, crawl in bed, turn our face to the wall, and not eat. If we can't have what we want, we sulk. We can sulk a long time, sometimes, can't we?

What we are doing is turning all those negative feelings inward. Disappointment, nurtured long enough, turns into anger, depression. These feelings eat at our insides, even literally, until our inner self is horribly misshapen.

Yes, though we may sulk around others, it is we who are emotionally, spiritually, and physically the greatest victims. And I say that is a terrible way to waste a disappointment.

LETTING GO OF DISAPPOINTMENT

What secret did Paul know that allowed him to rob disappointment of its power to defeat? Can we, like Paul, reshape each setback into a growing experience? Indeed we can.

The first step, I believe, is to *unlearn* some of the unhealthy responses we make when something we want is denied or taken from us. When our hopes are blocked, it is time for a self-evaluation.

Why not take a "disappointment inventory" right now? Ask yourself, What is my threshold of disappointment? What are the relationships, possessions, or positions that, if taken from me or denied, would bring disappointment—maybe even bitterness?

Maybe you are feeling disappointed about something right at this moment. If so, let these questions work inside of you: did I want the right thing? As I tried to attain it, were my methods right? Was my motive right?

Had Ahab taken this kind of personal inventory, he might have recognized that he cherished a piece of land more than a man's life. He would have seen, in the same way that we can see if we are honest, how values can become twisted, how our desires can sometimes become as idols.

Disappointment, when viewed in the right light, can expose our true values and motives. Success doesn't cause us to examine our inner selves the way a letdown can. We misuse those hard experiences if we don't see them as opportunities to replace wrong or misdirected goals with right ones.

Paul says, in 2 Corinthians chapter 4, that our present problems are meant to prepare us for a greater "eternal weight of glory." In effect he says, "These troubles we all face are transitory. They're going to disappear. We must set our eyes on eternity and that which doesn't change."

Maybe you are feeling disappointed about something right at this moment. If so, let these questions work inside of you:
- *Did I want the right thing?*
- *As I tried to attain it, were my methods right?*
- *Was my motive right?*

In effect, he is telling us that we must learn how to let go of disappointment. Some of our troubles are frayed and worn because we've been holding on, fretting over them, fingering them again and again until we're in tatters. Some folks rehearse their "bad breaks" and missed opportunities over and over until they, themselves, are one big disappointment.

Whenever I think about disappointment, I remember the season when my high school football team was undefeated and we were playing "the big game." We were pitted against the Jesup Yellow Jackets, a tough team, for the regional crown. What a battle that was! Both teams had tough defensive squads, and neither of us had come close to scoring the whole game. Near the end of the fourth quarter, we were still tied 0–0.

Now, there is trick play known as "the center sneak." The success of this play is that it works on split-second timing and it is rarely used. The center, who never runs with the ball, hikes to the quarterback, who immediately touches the ball to the ground. According to a little-known regulation, the center is then eligible to pick up the ball and run. It works once in a while.

In the final moments of that game against Jesup it did work—for them. The center snuck the ball past our middle-linebacker, crossed the goal line, broke the tie, and won the game. He was named "player of the week" by the *Atlanta Constitution*. My team lost—not just a game, but the regional championship.

And that was not the worst of it.

The guy playing middle-linebacker, the one who was supposed to have tackled the ball-carrier, was me. The center ran right by me, and I never touched him. I didn't even know he had the ball until I saw him jumping up and down with it in the end zone. He was a hero throughout the whole state—and I was the goat.

Talk about wanting to go home, crawl into bed, and turn your face to the wall! I not only *felt* disappointment, I felt I *was* a disappointment.

I admit, it took a long time to let go of that one. The feeling haunted me every time I walked into the locker room.

From that experience, and others that were far worse, I have learned to heed the advice of a music director I knew who was forever repeating this instruction to his choir: "When you finish a note, let it go cleanly. Then it has a beautiful ring to it."

In a similar way, we can learn to let go of disappointments cleanly. We can do this in prayer by saying, "Lord, it's over and done. All of my fretting and agonizing cannot change a thing. But by your grace and mercy I'm letting go."

LETTING GO OF NEGATIVE EXPECTATIONS

If we don't let go of the past, it will live to haunt us far into the future. We begin to live, not just with sorrow about hurts gone by, but we develop an expectation that the future will be a letdown, too. Everett Hale, the Boston clergyman and author, talked about the three kinds of troubles people bear. He said that some people bear the troubles they *have had*, plus the troubles they *now have*, plus all the troubles they *expect to have*.

When we bear all the troubles of the past, present, and future, we become sour, bitter, and cynical. Not only do we darken the day for everyone who has to live with our constant pessimism, but even worse, we will waste the great gift of life that is ours.

One person I knew who was a master at borrowing trouble from tomorrow was referred to by everyone who knew her as Sister. Thirty years before, Sister, who was loved by everyone in the community, had heard a sermon in which the preacher quoted a statistic—where he came by it was never clear—that more old people died in February than any other month of the year.

Sister was in her sixties when she heard this sermon, and in reasonably good health. But she went home that day and determined that the very next February she was going to die.

From that time on, whenever February rolled around, Sister would take to her bed. She became dreadfully ill and had to be waited on. The family even called that preacher and told him what his comment had done. He apologized for ever planting that idea in her head and asked what he could do to help. They said, "How about coming over to nurse her during the month of February?"

I knew and loved Sister. Many a time I visited her in February, that month she so dreaded. Each year, she just *knew* it would be her last. Just recently, she did pass away. And no surprise to those of us who knew her, it happened in February. The sad part was that she spent all those years expecting the very worst to happen to her every February for almost *forty* years—for Sister died at 101!

Negative expectations can get planted in our minds, and we allow them to root. In Sister's case, she seemed to go out of her way to water that expectation, too. Finally, she did indeed reap the harvest she expected.

Some may argue that there was a kernel of truth in the statistics that preacher had quoted. But it was a matter of what she *did* with that kernel.

I like to think about Kenneth N. Taylor, the man who gave us *The Living Bible*. For the benefit of his own children, Taylor spent years paraphrasing the Bible a little bit at a time. When he finished, he recognized that there might be value in his work that could benefit others. So he offered it to a publisher.

Immediately, he was turned down. Taylor offered the idea to another publisher. Again he was turned down. Not only that, but he was told, "Christians will never accept this kind of treatment of the Holy Bible." He went to thirty-six publishers, all of which turned him down. He was told to expect failure as long as he pursued such an idea.

But Taylor did not take that negative expectation to heart. Instead he did what he had to do: he formed his own publishing company and called it Tyndale House. Today, it is a fine company and, through it, Taylor has sold over 500 million copies of *The Living Bible*! It has been published in dozens of languages and has helped to spread the good news about Jesus Christ around the world.

Even though many professional publishers told him to expect disappointment, Taylor took his initial rejections and let them become a motivating force. In doing so, he redeemed the disappointments and turned them to good.

LIFE'S BLOWS NEED NOT BE DEFEATS

It is true that life's blows are not defeats unless we refuse to let God help us redeem them. He is the supreme Master of taking the letdowns of life and making something good out of them. I have this on good authority, from good friends like the Baileys, who have gone through potentially crushing circumstances.

Vermelle had been a friend since high school. So when Jean and I took a new pastorate in their community, it was natural that Vermelle and her husband, Ralph, should join our church. Deeply committed to the little congregation, the Baileys assumed huge responsibilities. She was the organist for every service; he was the choir director, the lay leader, and the adult Sunday school teacher.

Greater than their love for the church, however, was their desire to start a family. So the whole congregation rejoiced when Vermelle became pregnant.

Months later, on the night Vermelle entered the hospital to deliver, the waiting room was full of friends who had come to share in the Bailey's happiness. When the doctor came out with a stony expression and asked me to come with him to the delivery area, however, we knew at once that all was not well.

Standing at their side, I watched helplessly as Ralph and Vermelle's tiny, newborn daughter struggled feebly for life. She lived only a few minutes. Vermelle wept inconsolably, and Ralph plowed through the crowded waiting room to find a dark place outside to weep alone.

In the weeks after, we were all disappointed when Vermelle grew more and more bitter and finally pretty much dropped out of the life of the church. Ralph stayed, but his struggle was hurtful to see.

Eventually, Vermelle did return to the church and about the same time became pregnant again. During those months of waiting, we saw their new excitement replace the pain. Their faith grew. In fact, they responded to a call to the ministry, sold their home, quit their jobs, and went off to seminary.

When their son was born, it appeared that the Bailey's story would have a fairy-tale ending after all. Although Vermelle had to have an emergency hysterectomy a few days after the delivery, she was otherwise in good health and made a remarkably fast recovery. Their inability to have another child did not seem to concern them, because they were grateful and overjoyed with their long-awaited child, Michael. Then the worst happened.

Several days after Vermelle came home from the hospital, she was rocking the baby in her arms. For some unexplainable reason, Michael suddenly stopped breathing. No efforts could revive him.

When news of the baby's death reached us, Jean and I drove to be with our friends, greatly dreading what we would find.

When Ralph and Vermelle met us at the door, however, we saw immediately the remarkable calm that held them together. Of course, they were almost blind with grief. But this time something had changed inside. They told us, almost at once, "We know that God has two very special children out there for us to adopt. We're going to find them."

The Baileys did find two very special children, Cathy and Bill, whom they adopted. That was some years ago, and last year, Ralph and Vermelle became proud grandparents. They are still in the ministry, and I can think of no couple better equipped to console others in their loss. For they learned how to let God turn disappointment into joy.

INNER TRANSFORMATION THROUGH GOD

Do you have any doubt that our Lord is able to accomplish that inner transformation? Consider the fact that Jesus had poured more than three years of his life into a particular band of men—only to have one of them betray him and most of the others abandon him in his time of most urgent need. Yes, even that tremendous letdown was borne to the cross of Calvary, where Jesus showed the world for all time that every disappointment can be redeemed by the hand of God.

This, I believe, was the secret that Paul knew. This was the inner transformation that allowed him to defeat disappointment. Paul learned to let go of disappointment, "forgetting what lies behind" and forging ahead. Then he gave God room to work in any situation, no matter how dismal it looked, and so redeemed some crushing occurrences.

Just look at the final segment of Paul's life. He longed to preach the gospel in Rome, and even beyond into Spain. But Paul didn't get to Rome the way he intended, boldly declaring Jesus Christ in the great Forum. Instead, he was led down the Appian Way in chains, a prisoner of Caesar. He lived out his days under arrest, far from his native land.

Yet from that prison flowed the most triumphal letters to the infant Church, which still inspire and lift us nearly two thousand years later. Those letters, now part of our New Testament, have gone far beyond Spain, which Paul never reached, into all the world, converting millions. Likewise, during his life, Paul never preached in the Forum, but his words and his demeanor converted the guards in Caesar's household. He joyously proclaimed, "Because of me, the brothers and sisters here have lost their fear of chains!"

Are you still bound by disappointment—past, present, or future? Don't let it control you and keep you down. Use the secret of Jesus, Paul, and folks like the Baileys for yourself.

Take those disappointments and let them shape you in strength and compassion. Let them move you on to a higher place.

6. "One of *Those* Days . . ."
From Frustration to Freedom

Recently, I heard a story about a first-grade teacher who was having "one of those days."

To begin with, it was rainy. That meant the schoolchildren couldn't go outside to the playground. There seemed to be an excess of name calling, crayon swiping, pinching. By midday, the room was like a pressure cooker. The poor teacher thought three o'clock would never come. When it did come, at long last, she had to wrestle thirty wiggling bodies into raincoats, and sixty feet into rubber boots. But the end was in sight.

When she came to the last little boy, she tugged and tugged to get a pair of too-small boots on his feet. Just as she stood up again, the boy said, "Teacher, these aren't my boots."

Biting her tongue, hard, she dropped to her knees and laboriously yanked them off. "All right," she asked, straightening her aching back, "whose are they?"

The boy grinned. "They're my sister's—but I have to wear them."

We can all chuckle at a story like that. And the reason is we see ourselves in it. Certain things can really get us down.

But what about those situations in which we find ourselves blocked, pushed aside, or let down time and again? What happens when the world seems to be turning in the wrong direction? There are disappointments, some of them deep, which we considered in the last chapter. But what about those people we must live with who are impenetrably thick-headed, or circumstances that we won't change and can't be dodged?

What are we to do when the sense of frustration builds and we feel we are going to explode? How can we get a handle on frustration before it gets a handle on us? How can we turn it and shape it to our advantage?

Jean and I have experienced such feelings, as I'm sure you have at one time or another.

One time, burglars broke into our home. The sense of helplessness and of having our privacy violated was bad enough. But, among other things, they took our silver—not just the brand new silver we'd been given when we were married; they took monogrammed silver that had been in my wife's family for generations. For that reason, it was precious to us, irreplaceable.

The police gave us no hope of ever seeing it again. We felt terrible. It was a small consolation when our insurance company replaced the old silver with a brand new set.

Before we got it out of the plastic, however, thieves broke in again—maybe even the same ones!—and *that* set went, too.

This time, our outrage was unlike anything we'd felt before. Our home and our privacy had been ransacked *twice*, and there was nothing we could do about it. More than that, we sensed for the first time what a tangled mess our legal system is in and how out of control is the increase of crime in our country.

That was when I learned more about the root problem of frustration. It's not just that things sometimes work against us. Frustration comes from the realization that our private world, which we like to order and manage, is really beyond our control.

When that kind of frustration comes, chances are we're not chuckling. We're probably gritting our teeth, losing our temper, working on an ulcer, and generally having a bad time of it. The most maddening thing is that frustrations have a way of coming along at the very moment when it's *imperative* that life be smooth and orderly.

Consider, for example, the final weeks of Jesus' work on earth.

For about three years, he had tramped up and down the hills of Israel, speaking to people who showed a remarkable insensitivity to his teachings. One day he might teach his twelve rough-and-ready companions about serving one another, and the next day he would have to break up an argument about which of them would be greatest in his kingdom.

And then there was Peter, the one Jesus was counting on to pull his little band together and lead them. In Matthew's Gospel, we read that Peter finally had his eyes opened to Jesus' true identity. He exclaimed, "You are the Christ, the Son of the living God"

(Matthew 16:16). Then, only moments later, Peter tried to stand in the way of Jesus' getting to Jerusalem—an action that caused Jesus, in frustration, to call him a devil. Would these men never change?

For months, our Lord experienced the ultimate frustration of trying to train the unruly human heart. As his time on earth grew to a close, there must have seemed so much that was yet to come together. I can imagine the sense of futility that must have grabbed at him. Almost, you can sense the fraying of his nerves, especially in one very trying episode.

Jesus had climbed a mountain, we read in chapter 9 of Mark's Gospel. He was accompanied by Peter, James, and John. There on the heights, in a mystical experience beyond rational comprehension, he spoke face to face with two great men: Moses, the law-giver, and Elijah, the father of prophets. The meeting signified that Jesus, the key to humanity's redemption, was about to take his place beside them in glory and in history. What a moment!

What happened next?

Immediately after the transfiguration, Jesus came down from the mountain to find complete confusion. A man who brought his son to Jesus' disciples to be healed had found that they hadn't a clue as to how to handle the problem.

I can easily envision Jesus' arms dropping to his sides, staring at his men, only to get a "don't-look-at-me-it-was-his-fault" kind of response.

Sure Jesus could heal the boy himself, which he did. But that was not the point. These were the men he was counting on to spread his kingdom to the ends of the earth. He had entrusted to them the very Word and the healing power of God, and still they were botching things up royally. And time was getting short.

Can't you feel his frustration at months and months of thick-headedness? Can't you just see him throwing his hands up? Once before, he had said, "Don't you have eyes? Can't you hear what I'm saying?" Now he cried, "How long do I have to bear with you?" I wonder if, in that moment, he almost longed for Calvary.

The disciples remind me of the man who was always gung-ho when it came to his church's annual revival. Every year, the church had its tent meeting. And every year he would walk the "sawdust trail," fall to his knees at the altar, and get converted. Then no one would see him again until the next tent meeting.

One year, he went through his routine. Kneeling at the altar rail, he wept loudly. "Fill me, Lord. Fill me!" he cried.

Someone in the back apparently had had enough. And a voice called out, "Don't do it, Lord. He leaks!"

We, like Jesus, meet those frustrating folks all the time, don't we? They are everywhere—in our families, on the job, in church. It's a big challenge to live in a world full of frustration and still function effectively with a degree of fulfillment.

God did not intend for us to pull into a cocoon and withdraw from problem people. He does not want us to run from the things that get in our way and drive us up the wall. He allowed his own son to be a living example.

HOW JESUS HANDLED FRUSTRATION

How did Jesus handle frustration? As I study his life, I can see that he approached it from four angles.

The first approach Jesus used was quite simple: he verbalized his frustration.

We have some funny ideas about spirituality, don't we? One of them is that Christians should never show anger or frustration. A *true* Christian is always supposed to hold his or her tongue, always supposed to walk on a cloud above difficulties, with a beatific smile firmly in place. It's true that we aren't supposed to let angry frustrations rule our heart. But then what do you do when something really bothers you?

On more than one occasion, Jesus let his feelings spill out in words. Just before his crucifixion, we read that Jesus climbed a hill overlooking the city of Jerusalem, where he had been rejected again and again. You hear the longing in his voice as he says, "O Jerusalem . . . killing the prophets and stoning those who are sent to you! How often would I have gathered your children together as a hen gathers her brood under her wings, and you would not!" (Matthew 23:37).

Just as Jesus verbalized his frustrations, you and I cannot bottle up the things that disturb us in the name of some false kind of "holiness." The truth is, we are supposed to handle our frustration wisely.

I suggest that one very good way to get out your frustrations is to find a good friend, a pastor, or a counselor with whom you can share anything that's on your mind. Even the most unbearable problems come down to size when you can talk about them in the presence of a caring, listening friend.

One very good way to get out your frustrations is to find a good friend, a pastor, or a counselor with whom you can share anything that's on your mind. Even the most unbearable problems come down to size when you can talk about them in the presence of a caring, listening friend.

Once I heard Elie Wiesel, the noted author and survivor of the holocaust, speak. He had lost his parents and his grandparents in a concentration camp. Yet he managed to come out of that terrible experience with his sanity, while many others were deeply crippled in their emotions. He said that he discovered something crucial while in that hell-on-earth. For those who let out their anguish, who wept, it was easier in the long run to keep their emotional equilibrium. And it was those who could not or would not weep who most often became emotionally unstable.

There is a scripture that could do wonders for many of us when we're upset. Psalm 30:5 says, "Weeping may endure for a night, but joy cometh in the morning." There is great wisdom here. Once we allow that inner dam of pent-up frustration to flow, inner freedom can come.

Second, Jesus changed the things he *could* change. Consider again his encounter with the disciples who couldn't heal the little boy. At that moment, those men appeared to be quite hopeless. He'd done everything he could to teach them, to show them he was Lord. He had tried to challenge their faith into action. Jesus might have turned and stomped away from the lot of them. After all, the world was waiting for him to go up to Jerusalem where salvation history would be written.

Instead, he turned his eyes upon a helpless, hoping father whose little boy was hurting. He stretched out his hand of compassion one more time.

Do you know what it is that *really* gets us down? It's the backlog of little duties left undone. It's the accumulation of little "rubs" that should have been dealt with the moment they happened. Instead, we allow problems to grow and people to goad us, until one more little annoyance makes the lid blow off.

Jesus did not allow that kind of build-up. We, too, can make ourselves focus on the problem at hand. We can train ourselves to shut out what has yet to be done. Marvelously, almost miraculously, we find that the Lord then gives us the strength to handle each problem situation. And then the next. Perhaps we even find that our frustrations fall, one by one, when we attack them singly and not all at the same time. We may discover, in fact, that life is not so unmanageable after all.

But what about those situations that simply refuse to change, no matter what?

Jesus' third principle for handling frustration was, I believe, an ability to keep frustration in perspective.

When his disciples would shake their heads over things that, to them, were beyond comprehension, Jesus would say, "Look, there are a lot of things that seem impossible now. But relax. With God all things are possible" (see Matthew 19:26).

What I'm saying is that Jesus learned to face frustration with an accent on the *up*beat. He acknowledged how terrible things could be, he changed what was changeable—but he *always* kept a positive, hopeful, and expectant attitude about him. In the same way, we must reeducate our minds and moods until they conform to Jesus' example.

I have a friend I always run into at the YMCA. During the winter, when it's cold, he complains bitterly. Last spring, on a beautiful, warm day, I bumped into him and couldn't miss the chance to say, "Great day, isn't it?" He shook his head and replied, "Yes, but it won't last."

We have taken the words "yes, but" and used them exactly in the wrong way. Look through the New Testament sometime, and there you'll encounter the "reshaped" attitude of those who had taken on the Spirit of Jesus. They say, "Yes, James has been killed and Peter and John are in prison—but the word of the Lord is spreading throughout the world." They say, "Yes, we've been knocked down, but we aren't knocked out!"

People who encounter Jesus learn how to turn around "yes, but" until they have a firm grasp on God's eternal perspective. The great social commentator, Simone Weil, stated it another way. She said that the essence of faith is to wait with expectancy.

STAY IN A POSITIVE RELATIONSHIP

You say surely there is more to facing the "impossible" frustrations than keeping a positive attitude. Yes, there is.

The fourth and most important key of all is to stay in a positive relationship with God.

In a book called *The Town Beyond the Wall* by Elie Wiesel, there is a character named Michael who has been in prison for some time. In one scene, Michael is talking to a believer who asks how he has kept his sanity while being locked up so long. Michael confides his secret: he has found a true friend with whom he can share his inmost thoughts and hurts and hopes. By finding that kind of companionship in such stifling circumstances, he has kept himself together.

At that moment, Michael sees a knowing look in the eye of his visitor, which infuriates him. An atheist and proud of it, Michael quickly says, "Don't try to tell me that God sent this friend to me in prison."

The believer replies, "No, I won't tell you that. My God doesn't send people to prison. He goes himself."

Are you feeling imprisoned by frustrations? Do you feel that there is no one to listen to the cries of your heart? Let me assure you that Jesus Christ is reaching out to you right now with compassion. He says, "Come to me, all you who are weary and burdened, and I will give you rest" (Matthew 11:28).

Are you tired, frustrated? Jesus bore the cross of frustration all the way to Calvary. You need not "tie a knot and hang on," or bear frustrations with the stiff muscles of the stoic.

With his Spirit renewing your mind and with him walking beside you as a friend and confidant, you need not carry it any longer. You need not give in to mere stoicism. You can learn to meet unbending people and face obstacles with the expectancy that you will one day overcome. Begin today to make changes, and you will find within a new freedom.

In these last few chapters we have talked about getting into a right relationship with God, and then joining with him in forging a new relationship to the people and events that often hassle us and rob our joy.

We have yet to consider another area: the moral challenges that face us. By that I mean doubts, fears, depressions, and temptations that seek to batter our faith and our spirit until it becomes like a misshapen and useless vessel. These fires, too, can be used wisely in the process of reshaping a new you—if you know the proper spiritual tools that are available.

It is to these challenges, the ones that tear at the moral fiber of our souls, that we now turn.

7. The Long Step of Faith
From Doubt to Deepening Faith

Sometimes we collide head-on with deeply personal issues and moral dilemmas that are ours and ours alone.

One such dilemma can come when we are challenged and must call upon our faith—only to find that our supply seems woefully inadequate.

As a pastor, I've been asked countless times—as I'm certain others have—the following questions:

"I'm not sure I have any faith at all. Where does faith come from?"

"My faith is so small—where do I find more?"

Behind these queries lies a supposition: faith is a commodity that can be measured. Some people think that, within each of us, there is a well or repository into which faith can be poured—if only we can find the secret spring from which it flows. We imagine, some of us, that faith comes from *outside* of ourselves.

The truth is, most of us feel we do not have sufficient faith—whatever that substance is—to handle life's challenges.

In the previous chapter, we looked at Mark 9 and Jesus' encounter with the pleading father from the Savior's perspective. Now, we must look at it again, this time from the viewpoint of the father whose son was in need of healing. At once, we meet a man who was grappling with questions about his faith.

Evidently, the Gospel writers considered this an important story, for both Matthew and Luke record it as well. It is important to us because, in this man's moving encounter with Jesus, we hear our own questions asked and we gain some illuminating insights.

Mark reports that the father brought his boy, who had been made dumb by an evil spirit, to the disciples. Without warning, the spirit sometimes seized the boy and threw him to the ground. The poor child would foam at the mouth, gnash his teeth, and become rigid. Today, the boy might be diagnosed as having epilepsy. We already know the man had asked the disciples to pray that his son be healed, but they were unable to help. Then Jesus walked into the scene. But before we reenact their face-to-face encounter, let's examine some of the dynamics more closely.

This man began with some amount of faith. Hadn't he brought his son to the disciples and even pushed his way through a crowd to get to them? He came expecting to get help. Yet the moment his hopes were raised, the disciples failed to produce.

How many people have given up on the church or on Christianity because they've been disappointed by one of the Lord's followers? I'm sorry to say I know lots who have done just that. Is there some area of your life in which a fellow Christian has disappointed you? Has that bitterness seeped into your relationship with Jesus Christ, tainting your faith in him? Not so this desperate father. Jesus came up, and the man did not turn away but rushed to his side.

In this act, in his willingness to pick up and try again, it must have been obvious to Jesus that he had a measure of faith. In Matthew's account of the same story, Jesus may be looking that man in the eye when he says, "Truly, I say to you, if you have faith as a grain of mustard seed, you will say to this mountain, 'Move from here to there,' and it will move; and nothing will be impossible to you" (Matthew 17:20).

Most of us get hung up on the challenge of the mountain and forget the mustard seed. For Jesus was saying, "Look, it doesn't take a lot of faith. Start with the faith you have already. If you do, there's no limit to what can happen."

TAKING THE FIRST STEP

Do you feel that your faith is small?—or that you need more of it? Our Lord, apparently, expects us to use the measure of faith that we already have before we are given more.

Unfortunately, so many of us treat faith the way squirrels treat acorns. We want to store it up and watch it grow and grow. But that isn't the way it works. If you're waiting to become a great person of faith before you launch out and do the thing you believe God wants you to do—whether it's teaching a Sunday school class, or making a career move—chances are you'll never take even the first step.

The Bible is loaded with incidents that underscore this "first-step principle."

In Exodus 14, the people of Israel were terrified to learn that Pharaoh and his chariots were pursuing them into the wilderness. Moses boldly announced, "Stand still and watch the Lord fight for you." But the Lord thundered in reply, "Why are you crying out to me? Don't just sit there. You go forward, Moses, and then the waters of the Red Sea will part." In other words, "Let me see your feet in the water, and then I'll act."

"Truly, I say to you, if you have faith as a grain of mustard seed, you will say to this mountain, 'Move from here to there,' and it will move; and nothing will be impossible to you" (Matthew 17:20).

Most of us get hung up on the challenge of the mountain and forget the mustard seed.

We see this same principle at work elsewhere in Jesus' ministry. To a group of lepers who had asked if he would heal them, Jesus sent the message, "If you'll go and show yourselves to the priests, you'll be cleansed." They set off down the road and were healed on the way. To a blind man, Jesus said, "Go wash your eyes in the pool of Siloam." Splashing his face with that water, the man received his sight. Another man asked that his withered hand be straightened, and Jesus said, "You stretch it out."

This is no small matter. Each of these people could have stubbornly insisted, "You move first, Lord. Show me that you're going to act. Then I'll have some faith in you." If they had refused in that way, none of them would have received an answer from the Lord. Instead, they acted on the faith they had, small though it might have been.

With these examples in mind, we come back to Mark 9 and the man who wanted Jesus to heal his son. Immediately, Jesus greeted him with compassion. He met this father at the point of raw, human need. Right before their eyes, the boy fell to the ground, writhing in one of those awful seizures. Jesus, with exquisite sensitivity, felt the pain of that father's heart.

"Tell me," Jesus asked the man, "how long has your boy been this way? Tell me what it's been like for you. I'll listen."

As I see it, this was the first time that father had met someone who recognized his personal need, as well as his desire to have his son healed. For there is no pain that can approach the grief of helplessly watching your own child suffer. And as he stared into Jesus' kind face, the dam broke.

"Lord," the man replied, "my boy has been this way since he was just a little thing. He's fallen into the fire and into water and nearly been drowned. It's been terrible to watch him grow up like this and not be able to help him."

In the presence of a kind, understanding friend like Jesus, we, too, can spill the hurts and disappointments of our soul. We can pour out our deepest need and ask him for anything. Sometimes having our prayers answered is as simple as that.

Scripture tells us elsewhere, "You do not have, because you do not ask" (James 4:2). Is that the problem? Are you afraid that Jesus doesn't feel the hurt you feel, that he won't see your need the way you see it? Rest assured, he does. Expressing your hurts honestly is also a part of using the faith you have already. In so doing, we give evidence of our belief that God is a compassionate listener.

Still another matter is revealed in their dialogue. After letting the man express his grief, Jesus asks, "What about your faith?"

The man replies, "I believe—but I also have doubts."

Now most of us don't find it too difficult to pour out our heart-felt needs to God. But do we believe that he wants to fuse his power with our faith and really *act*?

So many of us are afraid to be honest with God and admit we have doubts about his power and ability. You see, it's become a cliché to call someone a "doubting Thomas." Thomas, you remember, was the disciple who wanted tangible proof of Jesus' resurrection (John 20). I, for one, think it's about time that we stopped giving Thomas bad press and started applauding his honesty. What would we have lost had Thomas not aired his doubts and questions?

In another setting, for instance, Jesus told his disciples, "I am going away from you. You know the way to the place where I am going. And you'll join me there eventually." Most of them apparently stood there nodding, just as if they knew what Jesus was talking about, though they probably hadn't a clue. It remained for Thomas to blurt out, "Lord, we don't know where you are going. So how can we know the way?"

Because of such honesty, we have that marvelous statement by Jesus, "I am the way, and the truth, and the life" (John 14:6). Thank God for Thomas! He didn't know, so he asked.

The marvelous thing about people who are honest enough to ask questions is that they always speak for a multitude. When it comes to faith and unanswered questions, so many of us refuse to admit our doubts because we don't want to look foolish. But, as H. G. Wells put it, "Ignorance is the first penalty of pride."

We need not be embarrassed to stand with that father in his moment of need and say, "I have some unbelief, Lord. Can you help me?" It doesn't offend Jesus or drive him away when we admit doubt. He accepts us that completely. When that father came face to face with his mixture of belief and unbelief, Jesus said to him, "Yes, I am able to help your faith grow. Here is what you can do. Bring the boy to me."

In this, Jesus is saying to you and me, "Come closer to me. Walk into my presence." Faith grows when we are in his presence. Faith is never founded on a concern with intellectual conclusions or an insistence on evidence, but rather on a relationship.

A RELATIONSHIP WITH GOD

I learned a lesson about the kind of faith that is based on a relationship with God in my first quarter at seminary as I began my studies for the ministry. During that time, it seemed to me that all my professors were not adding to my faith, but making me question it. They had all sorts of rational arguments about who authored which books of the Bible and so forth.

Faith is never founded on a concern with intellectual conclusions or an insistence on evidence. Faith is founded on a relationship.

When I went home one weekend, I decided to try some of those arguments on my mother. In some way, I guess I wanted to see if I could shake that solid belief she'd always had. So I started by telling her there was no way that Moses could have authored the first five books of the Bible, the Pentateuch, because he couldn't have written about his own death, which we read at the end of Deuteronomy. On and on I went about biblical higher criticism. She just smiled and went about her business. She wouldn't be shaken, and it was rather maddening.

Finally, I realized that Mother *could not* be upset by my rational arguments because she had a relationship. She knew whom it was that she met in prayer—he was always there for her. In that friendship, faith was always growing.

From that experience, I first learned that there is something more important than having all the right answers. The most important question we must all answer when it comes to the matter of faith is this: do you love Jesus, and are you determined to follow him all of your life? We don't become Christians when we look at a list of doctrines and say, "Yes, I agree with these concepts." Christianity is a relational religion because we are related to a person—Jesus Christ.

CHOOSING TO BELIEVE

Again, getting back to Mark 9, we uncover yet another, deeper principle about the kind of faith that grows. It lies within the father's plea, "Lord, help my unbelief." He was saying, "I know that my will is involved in the process of faith. I have to decide: am I going to be a doubter or a believer? Lord, I choose to come down hard on the side of faith."

This is not a point to be taken lightly. Jesus knew exactly what this man was saying. He knew there was a wrestling match going on in this man's soul—and in the souls of each one of us today. Even when we become a Christian, our faith is not automatically full-grown.

Choosing to believe is so crucial because it determines whether or not we will receive the faith we ask for. We must all ask ourselves these questions: am I willing to have my faith grow—or am I really afraid that God might require more of me then? Will he ask me to step out too far from my "comfort zone"? How am I predisposed?

In one of the first churches I pastored, we held a week of revival meetings. We had an outstanding guest preacher and people were being touched by his messages. I noticed that a certain man came the first two nights, but from the third night on, he did not show up.

On Friday afternoon of that week, I saw him and said, "These are great meetings. Why did you quit?"

He shook his head. "To be honest with you, I had to quit coming because that man's preaching was getting next to me. He was beginning to reach me."

Have you drawn a line like that? Is your soul crisscrossed with reservations that you are not willing for God to step over? If your faith is not growing, maybe you've decided that you have just enough to make you respectable and you don't want any more. None of that risky stuff.

How about it? What is your stance? Paul said that a runner who wants to win presses toward the mark—that is, he leans toward the tape. That gives him momentum in the direction of his goal. Are you leaning toward doubting—or leaning toward believing? Does your faith have an object, a goal?

The father we've been reading about in Mark 9 had a definite goal: to see his son healed. Out of his grappling with faith and unbelief, he enabled a miracle to take place. Most of the time we focus on the miraculous healing of his son, which was certainly important. But let's not overlook the miracle that took place in the father's life of faith.

Of course, every one of us might say, "If I could see Jesus the way that man did, I'd know my prayers would be answered. Show me a dramatic miracle or two and my faith will grow, too!"

How is it that we always want our faith to be tightly wrapped, all questions and prayers answered, a lead-pipe cinch? When all is said and done, at the bottom of our souls, we really want hard evidence before we launch our grand adventure in faith. Little wonder that many of us spend most of our time standing still, like a train that never leaves the station.

George Mayo was a man who had great influence on my life when I was a young minister. George told me of an experience he had as a little boy in Waycross, Georgia, which gave him an insight that served him all his life.

There was a train track near George's home, and he would often stand beside it and watch the trains as they sped northward on their way to New York City. New York seemed like a dream town to George, a million miles off, as it would seem to any small boy in the deep south. He noticed that, from time to time, the engineers pulled their train onto a sidetrack and waited until a signal light turned green. Then they'd get back on the main track and continue on their long journey.

George tried to imagine what it would be like if the engineers could know that the lights were green all the way up the line. Then they could full-steam it straight to New York without ever stopping. Suddenly, it occurred to him: the lights are never green all the way to the end of the line. The engineers take one green light at a time, first one, then another, then another.

Are you, perhaps, the kind of person who wants to know that the whole track is clear and all lights are green before you will take the first step? Does fear of failure cause you to remain stock-still, with your foot firmly on the brake? If that is so, you may one day wake up with a heart full of regret for all that "might have been"—if only you had tried.

You see, it is not as though we *can* remain stationary and be safe. If we do not risk and take steps of faith, then the chance is good that we will sink, one day or another, into that living hell called regret. That is why we *must* be willing to take a step, even when there is only one green light ahead and we cannot see any farther into the distance.

I would add another dimension to George Mayo's anecdote: sometimes not even *one* of the lights is green. Sometimes it looks like we are driving full-speed into a brick wall.

That was the way Jean and I felt at one point when we faced a test of faith shortly after we were married. We were still in college and were praying that I would receive a student appointment to a local church. Not only was I eager for the experience, but, frankly, we needed the money quite badly. We prayed, we waited, but no appointments came through.

One morning, Jean drove me to the north end of the little town where we were living and still attending college. I got out, kissed her goodbye, and spent the next footsore hours going from one merchant to another trying to find a job. Nothing was available.

In desperation, I went to a factory on the edge of town and applied for a position on the only shift that had openings—the 11 P.M. to 7 A.M. shift. I was carrying a full load of courses, and my morning classes began at 8 A.M. My last class did not end until 3 P.M. Even as I shook hands with the personnel manager, I had a sinking feeling that I did not have the physical stamina to complete my studies and work the midnight shift, too. But there seemed nothing else to do, so I accepted the job.

On the day I was to begin my all-night job, I walked out of history class and met a district superintendent of the Methodist Church. He had been waiting in the hall to speak to me. It seemed there had been an unexpected opening at a church in his district. They needed someone immediately to take a weekend student appointment. The salary, I noted, was nearly the same as I would make on the night-shift job. But there was more! The church would provide us with full-time summer employment.

Needless to say, Jean and I accepted our new assignment with a great deal of thanksgiving.

You see, many people, with more dramatic stories than ours, can attest to the fact that God continues to move ahead of us, always making a way—even when we think we are headed for a brick wall. These are the experiences he uses to shape in us that immeasurable commodity, the treasure called faith.

The secret, then, is to move out—whether one light is green, or none are green. Faith is formed and grown by stepping out many times. Ultimately, we come to rest in God's complete reliability.

Have you asked Jesus to give you more faith? Are you willing to receive it? Are you, at this moment, willing to take the first step, to do the one thing God is asking you to do?

If so, you will be given more faith. You will grow from strength to strength in your inner being.

Jesus, who is "the author and finisher of our faith," has promised to lead you through the very experience of doubt toward a faith that moves mountains.

8. The Secret of Letting Go
From Fear to Trust

I know a woman who is terrified.

One day, I was seated at my desk when she came into my office. She was so agitated that she could not even settle back in the chair. She sat right at the edge of her seat, as if she was ready to leap up and run. Her eyes were almost wild. When I was able to calm her down a little, she told me, "I've come to the realization that I live from day to day afraid that I might be afraid."

With that kind of deep-seated fear strangling her, I knew she was in a lot of trouble. The anticipation, the dread, is itself a source of emotional hurt.

Looking at me closely, she asked, "Are you ever afraid?"

I told her the truth: "Yes, every time I preach."

By the look on her face, I knew she thought it strange that someone who stands before thousands of people each week to bring the good news of the gospel should be afraid. But the truth is that public speaking still frightens me. My palms get moist. My collar feels tight. Even when I've prepared my message well and know that so many people seated there in the pews are praying for me, in the moment that I step up to the pulpit, I feel afraid.

I told her I was well aware that my response to preaching did not make much sense. But in the first or final analysis, fear doesn't make sense. Most often, the majority of our fears are irrational, shadowy, hard to get a handle on. They don't yield to logical argument or lists of reasons of why we shouldn't be afraid.

In the weeks and months to come, I counseled with this woman whose greatest fear was fear itself. She became involved in one of our church's home sharing groups, where she received the support and encouragement of many Christian men and women. And during that time, I was able to share some of the steps that have helped me to handle my own anxieties.

Many of us deal with terrors, great or small, nameable and unnameable—about our children, our jobs, our health, our marriages. These anxieties are crippling and rob us of the joy of living. They press us, shaping our souls into a distortion of those strong, free, and restful spirits they were created to be.

I have good news, however. You need not be pressed in and molded by fear any longer. You can begin today to seize the terrors and anxieties and mold them into new strengths.

UNDERSTANDING THE NATURE OF FEAR

The first thing we must do is to start with a basic understanding of what we are up against. The irrational nature of fear is one characteristic. One of my first revelations about fear was taught to me by my father.

As a little boy, living on our farm in Georgia, I had one chore that terrified me. During the fall when my father had to mind the furnace in the tobacco barn until late in the evening, it was my responsibility as the youngest boy to take his dinner to him. Now the barn seemed a half-mile away, though it probably wasn't more than three hundred yards from the house. But, invariably, it was dark when I had to go out the back door and make my trip out there.

I remember still how frightened I was by all the bushes and shadows. Wind would rustle the fallen leaves, and I imagined all sorts of menacing, scary things lurking. In my mind, weird noises filled the night air. I'd walk straight as an arrow down the very middle of the farm road, keeping just as far away as I could from the monsters on each side. By the time I reached the barn, trembling, I was so frightened I could hardly breathe. And then I'd have to turn around and walk back through the dark again!

But then there was one special evening that I'll never forget. I was too proud to tell Dad how scared I was, but somehow he became aware of it. After he finished his dinner, he said, "I think I need to say something to your mother. Maybe I'll just walk back home with you this evening."

How grateful I was, standing at the door of that barn, facing the dark road, to reach up and grip his big hand in mine. On that trip home, every frightening thing stayed in its place—just because my father was holding my hand.

REACHING YOUR HAND OUT TO GOD

From this experience, I later learned my first important lesson about fear.

I have come to see fear as a creeping, destructive force. The more we dwell on our fears, the more irrational they become. They wheedle their way deep inside of us and become buried where we cannot get at them—much less understand where they came from in the first place. Then they become dangerous, life-dominating. They overshadow everything. Fear can make us physically and emotionally sick. That is why counselors today help their clients scrape painfully through layers of past experiences until they get to the bottom of their fears.

The climb out of fear's dark pit, however, doesn't *have* to be a painful process. The first step in reshaping this destructive force is as simple as reaching your hand up to God, just as I instinctively reached out to my own father.

Remember that Jesus himself had to go through times that were heavy with anxiety. Surely his final night in the Garden of Gethsemane was one of those times.

Jesus had a lot of horror to anticipate on that night. The religious authorities had not hidden their pure hatred for Jesus; it was well known. Just that week he'd stormed through the temple precincts, overturning the tables of the money changers, accusing the priests and scribes of making God's house a den of thieves. But they didn't repent; they eyed him with cold contempt. And in those looks, he'd read every torture their evil imaginations had in store for him.

As he knelt in the garden, Jesus surely knew something about the inner torment of fear. Gethsemane is located on the western slope of the Mount of Olives, across the narrow Kidron Valley from Jerusalem. A grove of ancient olive trees covers the hillside. Because olive trees live for hundreds and hundreds of years, some of those trees that stand there today may have been saplings in Jesus' time.

In the center of the grove there would have been an olive press. I have seen many olive presses like the one that would have been in Gethsemane. (The Aramaic word "Gethsemane" means olive vat.) One often finds olive presses in the biblical lands. On the top of each press there is a round stone with a large wooden beam through it, which would take two sturdy men to turn. The stone would be turned slowly, making it descend in corkscrew fashion onto a larger stone at the bottom, which had small grooves cut in it. In between, the olives would be crushed and torn beneath the relentless grinding of the stones, extracting the delicious oil and reducing the rest to dry, dead pulp. Jesus knew, on that night, that he was about to be ground down by the hatred of men.

The Scriptures tell us that Jesus, "being in an agony . . . prayed more earnestly; and his sweat became like great drops of blood falling down upon the ground" (Luke 22:44). He knew they wanted to put a purple robe on him, place a reed in his hands for a scepter, and mock him saying, "Hail to the king!" They wanted to spit on him, to hit him on the head, to see his flesh torn with the Roman scourge. They wanted to see him nailed to a cross.

If we want to seize and refashion our fear, we too must learn to trust again. When we put our hands in God's, he will make the shadows stand still.

I am firmly convinced that Jesus, kneeling in Gethsemane, realized his fear would never yield to rational thought processes. So he did something that was quite simple and yet quite remarkable: he reached out for the Father's hand. And he never let go through the whole, ugly ordeal. Even on the cross, at the very moment he was to face humankind's most dreaded enemy, Death, Jesus cried, "Abba," an Aramaic word meaning *daddy*. Then darkness could not overwhelm him. Indeed, he conquered fear so completely that his last prayer was like that of a child laying his head down to sleep: "Father, into your hands I commit my spirit."

If we want to seize and refashion our fear, we too must learn to trust again. When we put our hands in God's, he will make the shadows stand still.

The words of the old hymn "I Won't Have to Cross Jordan Alone" have often stirred me and given great comfort:

> Tho' the billows of sorrow and trouble sweep,
> Christ the Savior will care for His own;
> Till end of the journey,
> My soul He will keep,
> I won't have to cross Jordan alone!
>
> I won't have to cross Jordan alone;
> Jesus died, for my sins to atone.
> When the darkness I see,
> He'll be waiting for me,
> I won't have to cross Jordan alone!

LETTING GO OF FEAR

Something dynamic happens when we recognize God's hand is there for us in the darkness. Once we realize it is *always* there, we are ready to take the next step toward freedom. We are ready to make the great exchange. For along with taking his hand in trust, we must also learn to let go of that gripping fear.

Some time ago, our family took a trip in the West, where we visited Carlsbad Caverns in New Mexico. The vastness of those caverns and the beauty of the rock formations were astounding, but what captured my interest most was the lecture given by a ranger one evening on the life cycle of the bats that live there.

In the first place, bats bear their young live upside down on the ceiling of the cavern—some *eighty feet* up from the floor of solid rock. The tiny offspring cling to their mothers only momentarily before they climb out onto the rocky ceiling, where they hang. Below them, on the cavern floor, live ants and other insects devour the bats that are too weak to hang on and fall to the ground.

Now though they have survived the initial crisis of an upside-down, high-altitude birth, that's nothing compared to the next challenge. Once a baby bat has reached a certain maturity, it must risk letting go of the ceiling for the first time, stretching its wings. At that moment, the baby bat has eighty feet to fall—or fly.

But it must let go!

We can learn a lesson from the bats. It is one thing to say we want to take hold of God's hand, but if we are constantly hanging onto our fears, we will never be free of them. It is true that some of us have become well able to operate within boundaries outlined by our anxieties. In fact, some of us, if we are honest, would have to admit that our fears have begun to fit us like a comfortable old shoe. Like the bats, we must let go if we are ever going to learn to fly.

Once we let go and take hold of God's hand, we can become involved in a process that leads to our ultimate release.

LEARNING WE ARE BRAVE

I am convinced that we have an unrealistic idea about those we consider heroes in the faith. We have read about women like Esther, who courageously confronted a heathen king and saved the Hebrews from slaughter; we think about men like Moses, who was pressed between the terror of the Egyptians and the waters of the sea. Most of us imagine that these people faced moments of fear, in the words of the antiperspirant commercial, "cool, calm, collected."

Did they? Or were these people, perhaps, just a little further along in a process?

King David, for instance, is revered as a great hero of the Bible. Even his deeds as a young boy seem to indicate that he had extraordinary courage. He killed a lion and a bear, we are told, with nothing but a sling. And then he conquered the giant, Goliath, when the whole army of Israel was cowering in terror.

But I think we miss something. *Before* the field of battle, *before* Goliath, David faced smaller tests of courage. He had to learn to defend sheep before he was brave enough to defend the honor of Israel. David could fight the giant because he first fought the paw of the bear.

Here is my point: we elevate the bravery of others, but what about our own?

Maybe you don't think of yourself as brave. But I have a strong suspicion that you are. Each one of us can look back on our lives and remember times of threat, physical or emotional. We have all been made to hold on through the darkness, perhaps with some trembling, but also with a measure of strength. In short, we have experienced the same mix of human emotions that our great heroes have felt.

Why not try this for a change? Instead of comparing yourself unfavorably with those you consider brave, take your own experiences and shine them up. I have no doubt you will discover that you have survived numerous attacks by the lion and the bear.

Try this for a change: instead of comparing yourself unfavorably with those you consider brave, take your own experiences and shine them up. I have no doubt you will discover that you have survived numerous attacks by "the lion and the bear."

To me, every time I make it through a sermon without my knees knocking, that is an experience to hang on my trophy wall. To my friend, the woman who was paralyzed by fear, every day that she can do something as simple as walk out the door and drive her car to work is counted for bravery. Who knows? She and I and others with fears great and small may one day be able to conquer a giant! One step at a time, we are on our way.

We are, after all, involved in a marvelous transformation. It is not simply for our own benefit that we become stronger, free from the darkness of fear. Once we have begun to enjoy the light of that freedom, we can take part in the work of sharing that brightness with others.

I never shall forget one of those "light-bearers," a wonderful friend who helped me through a time of crisis.

For almost three years, I had been working on my doctoral degree. I had finally completed all the research for my dissertation. A crucial deadline was looming: I had to slug my way through piles and piles of notes and accumulated work and had to have my dissertation finished no later than a certain date. It would be day and night until the work was done!

To begin with, I felt exhausted. Then there was the duress of the impending deadline. To top it all off, I began to feel a numbing fear. This was the final hurdle in a long, long process. What if I'd come this far and then blew it right at the end? What if my research or writing was not acceptable? What if . . . ?

It was late in the afternoon when I heard the knock on my study door. There stood a dear friend, lugging a huge thermos of coffee! He came in, set down the thermos, and took a seat at the other end of my study.

"Bill," he said, "I know you're struggling with this thing. I can't say a word that will help with your work. I'm here with coffee. If you need conversation, I can talk with you—if not, I'll be quiet the whole time. But I'm here for the duration just to be with you."

All that afternoon I worked, and he sat there. Occasionally, I said something. Now and again, he brought me a cup of coffee. I continued working all through the night—and on into the next afternoon. He was there the whole time.

I completed my difficult work; I met the deadline. And I will never be able to recall that tough time without being grateful to that good friend who knew what a fearful task I had and came just to be there.

You see, once we become free of our own fears, we can look with compassion on others. And we can be there to say, "Yes, you can do it. It takes work, and I can't do that for you. But you don't have to be pressed in by fear. You can seize it and remold it into strength."

At whatever point you find yourself in overcoming fear, I assure you of one thing: you need never face the shadows alone. Even if you do not have a friend to stand physically at your side, our Master is ever walking with you in the darkness.

I invite you to put your hand in God's hand right now. Do it whether you *feel* that he is there or not. Simply say, "Father, into your hands I commit my fears. Free me from these anxieties that are trying to bury me. Let me walk bravely on, accomplishing your purposes. Use me in your larger concerns from this day forward."

He who is full of love and light is there to help you triumph.

9. Three Keys to Hope
Transforming Depression into Joy

If we were to draw a line representing a perfect balance in terms of moods and feelings, and then charted our emotional rises and falls, all of us would dip below that line at one time or another. And when our emotions sag, we experience a feeling we hear so much about these days, a fearsome emotion we have identified with that catch-all word, depression.

What is the nature of depression? Who does it affect?

THE NATURE OF DEPRESSION

Depression comes in varying degrees and may affect each of us differently. We may call it "the blues," or say that we are "feeling down." More painful is that ingrained, day-after-day grayness of spirit that is paralyzing. While we may feel free to talk about doubts or fears, one of the deadly traps of depression is that when you are depressed, the last thing you want to do is talk. And so depression can be a deeper, darker pit than spiritual doubt or anxiety, which we considered previously.

One problem depressed people have is people who are *not* depressed. It is very painful for a depressive person to be around someone who is "up" all the time. The brighter their smile, the darker our pit looks by comparison. But comparison is exactly the thing a depressed person must avoid.

If we were to chart everyone's mood swings on that pencil line that represents the perfect balance of emotions, we would quickly see that personalities vary greatly. On the one hand, there are those people with such sunny dispositions that—seemingly, at least—nothing can cloud their day.

I recall reading about a football coach whose team was having a losing streak. One game after another, his team fumbled away the downs, once or twice coming close to victory only to go down in defeat in the final moments. It was tallying up to a dismal, losing season.

Someone asked that coach, "How do you keep your spirits up?" He shrugged and replied, "I'm the kind of guy who, if I fell in a mud puddle, would get up and feel in my pockets for fish."

Some people are just optimistic by nature and practically nothing can dampen their spirits. Then there are those folks who are rather gloomy in their thinking, pessimistic by nature. My friend Charlie is like that.

Charlie came to see me some time ago, and I took him out in the car to show him all around the wonderful city of Houston in which I live. Happily, I showed him a new Family Life Center, which our church had just opened. Then I drove him out to a community called Highlands to show him our retreat house. All along the way, he listened and nodded as I talked enthusiastically about the busy, vibrant life of our church family.

If we were to draw a line representing a perfect balance in terms of moods and feelings, and then charted our emotional rises and falls, all of us would dip below that line at one time or another.

As we were traveling back across the city on our way home, Charlie said laconically, "Well, Bill, you're in your forties now."

I waited for something more, but nothing came. "That's right," I agreed, curious as to why he was bringing up my age just now.

Charlie went on. "Just listening to your schedule—all the things you're busy doing—you remind me of a lot of men I know who are your age. And they're dying like flies. It's really frightening, Bill. They're just falling out all over the place."

I can tell you, I didn't feel like running a race after that!

You see, one of the problems these poor folks face is that, usually unwittingly, they tend to spread their gloominess to others. Granted they don't mean to, but they do, and usually at just the wrong moment. I was in a position emotionally where I could handle my friend's negative comments. However, a friend of mine who was in the hospital told me about a similar experience when a woman came to visit her right before surgery.

The visitor stationed herself in a chair and surveyed the room, the flowers, and the get-well cards. Then in a pleasant voice she asked, "What's the nature of your operation, darling?" My friend answered casually that the surgery wasn't going to be all that drastic. Her cheery visitor sat bolt upright and her eyes got wide. "Oh, dear. Three other friends of mine have had the exact same operation. Two of them died and the other is still in intensive care."

People like that aren't dangerous to themselves, but they can be dangerous to those who have to live around them because they can give out such terrible feelings. This tendency to look at the world through a dark glass is one characteristic of depression.

Not all of us spread our inner gloom to others when we feel down. Perhaps a more common characteristic, one we have all felt, is the sense of being closed in, shrouded by the vague but real feeling that something is just wrong with life.

It was the sixteenth-century mystic Saint John of the Cross who coined the term, "The dark night of the soul." That is an apt, if somewhat chilling phrase. Georgia Harkness, a twentieth-century theologian, popularized the term, recognizing how applicable it is today for the many who, having dipped below the emotional line too long, find themselves burdened with radical personality problems.

Today, there is an epidemic of people who feel they are struggling emotionally. Not only do they feel they are in a pit, but that pit seems to be filling up with water. They flail their arms to stay afloat, they kick against the darkness of their soul, yet they never feel as though they are getting their heads above water. Nor is there a gleam of light toward which to swim. Most think their problems are unique in all the world and see no solution and no end to their struggle.

Depression has a different effect than fear, which we considered in the previous chapter. Fear seems to press you in, to limit you. Depression leaves you with the feeling that life has no shape at all. All is flat, meaningless, without hope.

THE ROOTS OF DEPRESSION: ELIJAH AND JONAH

We may well ask, how does a person come to feel this way?

There is a story in the Bible about classic depression. It involves the prophet Elijah, who was a great champion of God. We would do well to look at it in examining the issue. His story will help us to do two important things. It will expose some common reasons for depression (things so common, in fact, that we often overlook them). And it will place in our hands some God-given tools that any of us can use in the work of moving from depression to a healthy inner life.

In 1 Kings we read that Elijah did some amazing things. He stood up to Ahab, a king of Israel who turned against God; because of Elijah's prayers God withheld rain from the earth for three years; Elijah even went to battle with the evil prophets of Baal. He did everything God commanded him no matter how difficult or taxing.

But one day he came to the end of his resources. He sat under a broom tree, saying, "It's enough, oh God. I have run out of the will to live. I just want to die." We might say that everything in his circumstances had conspired to push him into nervous exhaustion. We can know this because the writer of Kings makes it a point to tell us that, immediately after this cry of desperation, Elijah laid down and fell asleep.

It's revealing that the first thing God did was to allow his prophet a good night's sleep. Then Elijah was roused from sleep to find that the Lord had brought him cakes and a pitcher of water. The Lord said, "Eat, Elijah." In other words, "Take care of your body." And after the prophet slept some more, the Lord sent him on a retreat.

As with Elijah, there is a good possibility that the depression many of us battle today may involve a physical problem, perhaps even requiring medical attention. Let's consider this for a moment.

With the busy, busy lives most of us lead these days, sometimes an overburdened schedule is the culprit. If our lifestyle is a detriment to good health, if our basic physical needs aren't being met—a balanced diet, enough exercise, and enough rest—and if we aren't listening to the good advice of our physician, then there is the likelihood that we are abusing our body. We can't expect God to intervene miraculously if the way we're living leads to the condition Elijah fell into—physical and nervous exhaustion. We must change our behavior so that God can join his efforts to our own in turning our health picture around.

Only after God made sure that Elijah had attended to all of his physical needs did he begin to talk to him about the matter of his depression. For Elijah had despaired, thinking he was the only one left in the land who was suffering under the rule of an evil king. Yet the Lord told him, "Elijah, you feel so alone. But I have seven thousand others who face the same circumstances. And my grace is sufficient for every one of you."

This gets at another cause of depression. Sometimes depression is rooted in mental and psychological conditions. I think of the statement by John Milton that the mind is in its own place and, in itself, can make heaven of hell or a hell of heaven.

For me, it's somehow helpful just to think about some of the great people who felt the way I sometimes feel. The Bible is filled with men and women who found themselves trapped in the same mental hell of their own mind, a hell into which modern men and women still fall.

Job, for example, said that he had been given worrisome nights when he tossed to and fro on his bed until the dawning. Do you remember that wonderful man Jeremiah? In his emotional anguish, he cursed the day he was born, saying, "Let no one bless the day when my mother brought me into this world." You and I have experienced those feelings, too, at one time or another.

Jonah, the prophet, is perhaps a more interesting character study. At the end of the book bearing his name, we learn about Jonah's desperate emotional state. He cried out, "God, I'm angry enough to die. It is better for me to die than to live."

Why did Jonah feel that was so?

Because God had shown mercy to the people of Nineveh when Jonah wanted him to bring down brutal judgment. In other words, Jonah wanted God to come around to *his* way of thinking, but God had his own way. So Jonah began steaming, building up anger and hostility, until he was so full of it that he wanted his own life to end. Perhaps it will be enough for some who are reading this to observe that, all the time Jonah was angry and depressed, God wanted the prophet to come around to *his* way of forgiving. Yes, unforgiveness is a prime cause of the anger that leads to depression.

HOW JESUS TURNED DEPRESSION INTO VICTORY

With that thought, we ought to examine Milton's wise observation a little more closely. For if your mind has the power to drive you into the hell called depression, then your mind also has the power to lift you out of it.

Nowhere in the Bible, or the rest of history for that matter, do we find one whose mind was turned to the positive, the good, the uplifting side of living more than Jesus. And he of all people, knowing the heart of humankind, surely had the potential for great depression. As the Bible says, he was tempted in all things (see Hebrews 4:15). Then he must surely have borne the cross of depression, too. The question comes immediately. How did he do it? How did he turn depression into victory?

I believe Jesus handled the depression that comes upon all men and women in three ways.

A LIFE SHAPED BY PRAYER

First, Jesus knew the secret of a life founded on prayer. That may seem too obvious a statement for anyone to make about the Son of God. Let me explain what I mean.

When we think about Jesus' prayers, as recorded in the Bible, we immediately think of two references. One is commonly known as the Lord's Prayer, which we find in the Gospels of Matthew and Luke. The other is Jesus' great priestly prayer for all believers as recorded in John's Gospel, chapter 17.

There were times, however, when Jesus' prayers were not so eloquent. They came from his lips as deep groanings, uttered at moments of tremendous emotional pain and longing, and welling up from the depths of his soul.

Consider the time he was summoned by his friends Mary and Martha because their brother Lazarus was dying. When he arrived at their home in Bethany, however, Lazarus was already dead. We know Jesus' immediate response, because every Sunday schoolchild is taught the shortest verse in the Bible: "Jesus wept" (John 11:35). Let's look more closely.

Jesus asked the mourners to take him to Lazarus' tomb. The Bible then tells us, "Jesus therefore again groaning in himself cometh to the grave" (John 11:38). There he lifted up his voice in a prayer that rings down through the ages: "Lazarus, come forth" (John 11:43).

We cannot separate Jesus' groaning and weeping, the pouring out of his soul's deepest feeling in the face of human anguish, from prayer. It was, in fact, perhaps one of his most powerful prayers. For it resulted in the raising of Lazarus from the dead.

The Apostle Paul also refers to this deep kind of prayer—which is what I call "primitive prayer." In Romans 8:26, Paul says that sometimes, when we don't even know how to pray for ourselves, the Holy Spirit prays for us with groans and "sighs too deep for words."

Have you ever considered that the very groans and sighs that come from your lips when you are depressed reach the ears of our heavenly Father as a prayer? That is what the Scriptures would have us know.

Moreover, when we groan from the depths of despair, we may be sure that God is as close to us and as attentive to our prayer as he was to the groanings of his Son, Jesus. And just as he raised Lazarus from the tomb, he is eager to raise us out of the living death of depression.

THE LIFTING POWER OF PRAISE

The second secret Jesus knew in overcoming depression was the lifting power of praise.

When we read the Gospels, we see Jesus as he walked those Galilean hills. Certainly there was a lot of human misery in Jesus' day. Nearly every day, outside the city of Jerusalem, men were crucified by the Romans and left to die. There was gross poverty, incurable illness.

Yet we see in Jesus a remarkable ability to thank God for the beauties of life, the wonders of creation. In Jesus' teachings, he pointed men and women to the lilies of the field and to God's loving care of the birds. He pointed out the commonplace creation to his disciples, saying, "Look at God's wonderful world. Isn't the Father good to give us all these things?"

The Bible shows us that now and again Jesus would spontaneously break forth with a doxology. Once, he publicly shouted, "I thank you, Lord of heaven, that those things you have hidden from the wise and prudent you have revealed to babes. Thank you, Father, for being so faithful to hear our prayers and for being so steady in your love for us."

We also learn that, just a short time before Jesus was betrayed, he left the upper room where he'd eaten the last supper—and he sang a hymn as he went. Jewish custom tells us that the hymn he sang was most likely the *Hallel*, which is the chant used in connection with the Passover meal. The *Hallel* encompasses Psalms 113 through 118. In the middle of that powerful hymn are the words, "When I was brought low, God rescued me. . . . The steadfast love of the Lord endures forever!"

There is a Chinese proverb that says, "If I keep a green bough in my heart, the singing bird will come." Jesus kept that green bough in his heart—the bough of praise for the goodness of God—no matter what was happening around him, whether human suffering or his own betrayal and torment. And always, the singing bird came.

If we have any doubt Jesus was identified by his overcoming attitude of praise, consider an incident that occurred after the resurrection. On the road to Emmaus, Jesus came walking alongside some of his own disciples who did not recognize him. He walked with them a long way, revealing much about the Scriptures. It is interesting that the disciples did not recognize their teacher as he taught them. When he stopped for supper with them at a small house in a provincial village, they had asked him to bless the meal. Something in the way he thanked God let the men know this was the Lord. Then came recognition: they knew him by the way he praised.

A PASSION FOR MISSION

Jesus' third secret of victory was *passion*—an all-consuming desire to complete the mission his Father had given him.

On the night Jesus was betrayed, he sang praises and he prayed in Gethsemane. But when the darkness came for him, when there was no time left to praise and prayer was interrupted, Jesus focused on his mission. He said, "Rise up, men. It's time to finish it—to drink the cup my Father has given me. I won't leave the mission undone."

I think Rembrandt captured some of Jesus' inner fire in one of his etchings that is on display in New York's Metropolitan Museum of Art. The great Dutch artist depicts Jesus driving the money changers out of the temple. It is most interesting to note that Rembrandt did not draw a halo around Jesus' head, but around his hand.

You see, there is a connection between the head, the hand, and the heart. People who have a mission know what that connection is. Because they have a high and holy purpose in living, they may get down, but they don't go as deep or stay down as long as someone whose life is without purpose. Not that everyone must be an overseas missionary or preach. But each of us needs to step out and find the task that draws upon every fiber of our being.

When we look at Jesus' life as a whole, a beautiful pattern emerges. He made sure that he had a quiet place to pray, he lifted up his own soul with spontaneous praise, and he was carried by a passion for the task God had given him. In this, I see a rhythm. In cultivating that rhythm, Jesus was never out of sync with God—whether in the silent wilderness of prayer, or in the bustling marketplace with clamoring, needy crowds pressing in on all sides.

STANDING ON THE ROCK OF GOD

Because Jesus knew how to interact with his moods, he could withstand the worst. When pain and struggle lay just ahead, he didn't panic, or give in to depression. Prayer, praise, and passion had taught him that, even at the very depths of life's experiences, there is a rock to stand on. That rock is God, our heavenly Father, who is always there, full of love, unchanging.

We, too, can cultivate that threefold practice in our lives. Then we are less likely to give way to self-pity and anger and all the other debilitating emotions that would drag us down to our destruction.

When we are struggling to escape the darkness of our own soul, it is so good to know that our Savior went before us, bearing the cross of depression, turning it to victory.

Having been to the bottom of despair, he can help us transform our inner darkness into a heaven of joy as no one else can. The pattern is laid before you.

10. You Can Win the War Within
From Temptation to Commitment

I was walking down Main Street in Houston some time ago, when I was startled by an unorthodox kind of sound. It was grating, metallic, very loud, and frighteningly near to me. Quickly, I stepped over to the edge of the sidewalk to see what was happening.

Just as I did, some doors in the sidewalk opened, and up came a freight elevator, the kind that carries cargo on an open platform. What I had heard was a warning signal to clear the sidewalk.

Since then I've thought it would be nice if we had an alarm system that went off when we are being tempted and sin is about to emerge from our lower nature. Unfortunately, we seldom know when temptation is going to come.

It was William James, the noted American philosopher, who said that no one is ready to graduate from the School of Life until he has been well tempted.

In some quarters today, the word *temptation* and its relative, *sin*, are considered archaic. There are those who maintain that we do not really have the freedom to choose right or wrong. From their humanistic viewpoint, they say we aren't responsible for our actions; we simply respond to stimuli in the world around us. Therefore, the man who steals bread may say, "I didn't steal it. It was my *hunger* that stole." In other words he may blame any influence—the fact that he was raised in a poor home, that his father was absent, that he is out of work—to legitimize this sin.

For these folks, their god is animal instinct. They are guided by their glands and they simply give in to whatever feeling is strongest at the moment. These folks usually don't feel too sorry about their lives—not until sin leads them into personal pain, that is.

But the Bible's view is clear. First, temptation is real. Second, God, who made us rational beings, holds us accountable for our moral decisions. Whether or not we yield to temptation is our choice. A few great people in our era were never duped into modernistic thinking, including William Jennings Bryan, who recognized that "destiny is more a matter of choice than chance."

YOU *CAN* OVERCOME TEMPTATION

Now it is interesting to me that, even among good, Bible-believing Christians, opinions about temptation vary. Quite often, I counsel those who believe they are powerless to overcome temptation.

"I'm just so weak," they say. "If God doesn't take over and fight the battle for me, I'm just going to give up and give in."

For some folks, temptation is very real and just too overwhelming.

On the other hand, I also encounter Christians who have exactly the opposite opinion. Some of us think we have settled into a privileged position so close to the Lord that surely the pull of sin will *never* affect us. To these good folks, I offer a warning: not even the Son of God was exempt from temptation—though he was without sin—nor are any of us.

The Apostle Paul wanted to impress the believers of his day with the truth about temptation's power. To illustrate his point dramatically, Paul related a little bit of the history of the people of Israel.

In 1 Corinthians 10, Paul reminds his readers that, during the exodus from Egypt, the Israelites lived "under the cloud"—that is, the Shekinah, the pillar of cloud that represented God's glory among them. These people saw the parting of the sea and walked between the waters as on dry ground. They were fed miraculously by God on manna; they drank water that spurted miraculously from a rock.

In spite of their closeness to the presence of God, however, and in spite of the miracles, they were tempted into unthinkable sins: the idolatry of worshiping a golden calf; fornication; and murmuring against God, leading to open rebellion in which 23,000 fell in one day. Perhaps the most insidious sin that Paul lists is the fact that they traded on the mercy of God. In effect, they said in their hearts, "I know it's a sin, but I'm going to do it anyway because I know God will forgive me."

With this tragic history in mind, Paul hastens to warn the Corinthians, and we who read this letter today, "So if you think you are standing firm, be careful that you don't fall!" (see verse 12). What profound insight into human nature Paul shows in that statement. How true it is that, just when we think we are really secure, we should beware.

What the apostle is saying is this: the price of victory is vigilance. Even if you're feeling the closest to God that you've ever felt, stay on guard. For in that moment the Temptor may come.

Witness the experience of Jesus. At his baptism in the Jordan River, the Holy Spirit settled upon him like a dove. The very sky opened and a voice from heaven said, "This is my son in whom I am well pleased." He experienced the strongest confirmation of his identity and of his life's mission—followed immediately by a time of great temptation in the wilderness. And during that struggle, Jesus learned more fully about the battle that rages over the souls of men. He could say, with every bit of authority, "Watch and pray, lest you enter into temptation."

Now there is another reason we must learn to be wary. If the Temptor came with a sinister look and the scent of brimstone, most of us would have no problem with temptation. We react quickly in the presence of obvious danger.

I still recall how totally unsuspecting we were one pleasant Saturday when my wife, Jean, and I went canoeing with another couple. The current was lazy and the sun made the blues and greens more lush. Our friends were in a canoe behind us.

At one point, the water began to move swiftly, carrying us through a curtain of overhanging willow branches. We ducked and dodged our way through, unable to see what lay ahead. Just as we'd cleared the trees, I looked over my shoulder to see if our friends would make it.

To my horror, the woman was just reaching for a branch, and on it, hidden from her view, was a deadly water moccasin.

"*Snake!*" I shouted, pointing wildly.

Her eyes bugged, and she jumped out of the canoe into the river. At the same moment, the moccasin dropped from the branch into the water. When she came up, sputtering, I shouted again. *"It's in the water!"*

She jumped back in the canoe. I can't tell you how she did it. I don't think the canoe even shook. It was the fastest in-and-out of the water I've ever seen in my life. I wanted to touch her to see if her clothes were wet!

The point is, avoiding temptation would be a simple matter if the danger was as obvious as a water moccasin coiled on a branch. Unfortunately, it isn't. Sometimes it is subtle, and always it is appealing.

That brings us to the other side of temptation. We cannot always blame the Temptor, that voice *outside* ourselves. We also have to deal with our own lower nature. Paul, in Romans chapter 7, refers to the "war" that rages within each of us. Within our very soul, we wrestle between the desire to serve God and the desire to do what will make us feel or look good, even if it means damage or destruction. So we war *without* and *within*.

Recognizing that this battle goes on, however, we have a great advantage. As Paul instructed, we can learn how to be on our guard—that is, we can learn the strategy of vigilance.

There is a legend about a conversation between God and the devil. They were talking about a young woman who had always been strong and faithful. But she had just fallen victim to temptation.

The wise Christian knows that there are some situations he or she should not walk into.

Amazed, God asked Satan, "How on earth did you tempt her?"

Satan shrugged. "She wandered into my territory. After that, the rest was easy."

Being vigilant means to be honest with ourselves. That is our first defense.

The wise Christian knows that there are some situations he or she should not walk into. The inner voice may say, "Go ahead. You're strong enough to handle it." Don't be fooled! If you knew of a field that was littered with hidden land mines, and you knew others had walked there and been blown apart, would you risk it? Would you try to cross that deadly ground just for the satisfaction of saying, "That wasn't so bad"? If that's your thinking when it comes to temptation, then *beware!* The writer of Proverbs would call that pride—which always precedes a fall.

I like the advice of Sam Snead, the famous golfer. Someone asked him what he did whenever his ball landed in a sand trap or in the brush. He replied, "The best way to handle the rough is not to get into it." Sure, it sounds homey. But it's some of the best advice any of us can follow.

RUNNING FROM TEMPTATION

Now we don't always go out looking for trouble. Sometimes it comes looking for us. What do we do about those temptations that seem to come gunning?

Lately, here in Houston, we've had a rash of incidents in which dogs have attacked small children. As a result, the newspapers have run several stories about the attacks—some of which have been pretty gruesome. There was one, however, involving a little boy called D.J. that was not so tragic.

The reporter asked D.J. how he managed to come away from the attack unharmed. You can almost picture the serious expression on the little guy's face as he said, "Well, right in the middle of the attack, the Lord spoke to me."

(I'll bet the reporter's eyebrows shot up.) "Oh, really—he spoke to you? And what did God say?"

"He said, 'Run, D.J., run!'"

We always expect God to say something theologically profound, don't we? We make spirituality so complex—we want to ponder the inner workings of our soul, dissect the way temptation lures us, and know why, why, why we fall into the same traps again and again. And all the time God is saying, "You have two feet. If you're smart, pick them up and put them down. Don't stand there and analyze it. Run!"

If there was one man in the Bible who knew how to beat a hasty retreat from temptation, it was Joseph, whose story we find in the later chapters of Genesis.

When his brothers sold him into slavery, Joseph was taken to Egypt. There, he was bought by a wealthy man named Potiphar. We may make two assumptions about Joseph from what we read in the Bible. The first is that he must have been quite intelligent, for Potiphar placed him in charge of the affairs of his household. The second assumption we may make is that he was probably attractive—and that got him in trouble.

One day when Potiphar was not at home, we read, Potiphar's wife summoned the handsome young Hebrew and tried to lure him into her bed. Joseph refused. She seized his garment, probably a loose-fitting robe such as is worn in desert cultures, and tried to force him. But Joseph tore away, leaving his robe in her hand, and ran from her chamber.

Now stop and think about this for moment. Joseph had suffered quite a bit. He had lost his freedom and was a slave in a heathen land. Not only that, he was a young man in the prime of life, and certainly he must have had desires. And then his master's wife makes an offer. Maybe, if he went along with her, it could even lead to his freedom.

But the one thing Joseph did not do was to stop and think it through. For to reason with temptation is to lose.

Let me speak plainly: we must get it straight in our heart that temptation is a water moccasin waiting to bite; we must make up our mind to get away from it any way we can, as quickly as we can. That is our part. Until we come to that point, we are probably willing to play around with sin. Oh, we can *say* we want God to come along and help us, but we're only fooling ourselves.

THE WEAPONS OF SPIRITUAL WARFARE

When our minds are made up and our feet are moving, then God can do his part. As Paul said, "God is faithful; he will not let you be tempted beyond what you can bear. But when you are tempted, he will also provide a way out so that you can stand up under it" (1 Corinthians 10:13). In fact, God has already provided the weapons of our spiritual warfare—but only when sin is like poison to us are we ready to take up his arms.

What are these weapons?

One is the divine power that rests in the Word of God. Notice how Jesus dealt with the Temptor in the wilderness. Satan tempted him to turn stones into bread, then to do something spectacular like jump from the pinnacle of the temple so God's angels could save him. Then Satan promised Jesus the kingdoms of the world if he would worship at his feet. Each time, Jesus countered with the Word of God. And when he finally said, "Be gone," there was nothing else for the old Adversary to do but flee.

Paul reminds us several times in the New Testament that our spiritual equipment isn't complete until we know how to use "the sword of the Spirit, which is the word of God" (Ephesians 6:17).

The second weapon God hands us in our battle is named in Revelation chapter 12. There the Apostle John is writing of those who lived in victory despite crushing odds. What was the secret of their strength? He tells us, "They overcame by the blood of the Lamb and the word of their testimony" (see verse 11).

Once a very good friend, who works in a large firm, sought me out for help with a problem that was tearing him apart inside. When we sat down to talk, he laid out an explosive situation that could wreak havoc in his office, not to mention destroying his marriage and his home.

Struggling to speak, he explained, "There's a young woman at work that I'm attracted to—and she's attracted to me. She's married, too. We've already talked about our feelings. The pressure is building and building. I need you to help me, Bill."

I began to encourage him. And I could not help but ask, "What is it that's kept you from giving in to your desires?"

His reply came readily. "Some years ago, I accepted Jesus Christ as my Savior. I know that he suffered and died for me. When I think about giving in to sin—well, I just can't do that to my Lord. I don't want to hurt him any more."

That was not all. He quickly went on. "I've also made a commitment to my wife, and it's a holy commitment. I'm going to be faithful. I just don't know what to do."

I didn't need to hear any more. I had heard his heart. And I think he was a little surprised when I suggested, "Go tell this woman exactly what you've told me."

Days later, he contacted me again. The pain I'd heard in his voice was gone. Over a cup of coffee, he had told the woman about his Christian commitment. I have no doubt that it was difficult. But it ended the relationship that might have crippled many other lives.

And that was not the end of it. Some time later, largely because my friend told her about his commitment to Christ, this woman gave her heart to Christ, too. Then my friend had an ally there in the office, someone who was not out to destroy his commitments, but to help him keep them.

Yes, something powerful happens when we stand our ground and openly verbalize our faith in Jesus. When we stand for him, he stands up for us.

We have a third weapon in our war against sin and that is the fellowship and support of others.

It is not by accident that the New Testament speaks of the Church as "the body of Christ." God intends for us to be knitted together with others, not just to work on his behalf, but so that he can use others to work on *our* behalf in times of weakness.

Paul tells us,

> Brethren, if a man is overtaken in any trespass,
> you who are spiritual should restore him in a
> spirit of gentleness. Look to yourself, lest you
> too be tempted. Bear one another's burdens,
> and so fulfill the law of Christ.
>
> (Galatians 6:1–2)

If there is an area of moral weakness in your life, one of the worst things you can do is to try to conceal it. Instead, I recommend that you seek a pastor or a Christian friend with whom you can be honest. Tell this confidant exactly what it is you are tempted by. This kind of supportive friendship sets in motion an interesting dynamic within.

You may quickly find that the very act of verbalizing your temptation destroys some of its power over you. Kept in secret, temptation grows like a poisonous vine. Though we may think we are strong on our own, temptation is always waiting to trip us up.

You will also discover that friends can be more ruthlessly honest with us than we dare to be with ourselves. Treasure the friend who will not spare any words but will tell you to your face when you are dallying around with temptation.

Too many times, we think that we must be *nice* in order to be a Christian. Or we think that the Church is made up of nice people who talk about nice things. That kind of Christian fellowship may be pleasant, but it does not begin to approach Paul's instruction that we are to "bear one another's burdens."

Something powerful happens when we stand our ground and openly verbalize our faith in Jesus.

When we learn to rely on each other, to seek others who can identify with us in our weakness, who can both encourage and challenge us, we begin to discover one of the greatest truths about the Church of Jesus Christ. For it was he who said, "I will build my church, and the powers of death shall not prevail against it" (Matthew 16:18).

These weapons—the Word of God, the word of our testimony, and the fellowship of Christians—are invincible. The key is to shape a heart that will be vigilant, willing to run from sin if need be. When we do our part, and God does his, no sin can overtake us.

Christians through the ages have discovered this sure and valiant manner of dealing with the trials of faith. Listen to what Paul said to his young disciple, Timothy: "God did not give us a spirit of timidity but a spirit of power and love and self-control" (2 Timothy 1:7).

The Apostle John echoed Paul's words when he wrote, "He who is in you is greater than he who is in the world" (1 John 4:4). No temptation is bigger than the strength we can find within.

Martin Luther also knew about warring with temptation. And he knew of the victory that can be ours. The words of his triumphant hymn, "A Mighty Fortress Is Our God," resound:

> The Prince of Darkness grim,
> We tremble not for him;

His rage we can endure,
For lo, His doom is sure;
One little word shall fell him.

Do your temptations seem too big to overcome?

Recognize that God *has* given you the way of escape. It is as close as your heart, as simple as the words you speak, as close as your nearest Christian friend. Your ability to win is as sure as your commitment to Jesus Christ—and as solid as his commitment to you.

Perhaps, having read this far, you still find that some of your most fiery trials have not been touched upon. Maybe certain circumstances in your life seem wildly out of control. Maybe you or someone you dearly love is suffering. And what about that ultimate challenge, death? Who among us has not wondered, despite all efforts not to borrow trouble, how we will be able to cross *that* bridge when we come to it? There are times when it seems that the universe is an impersonal machine that is working against us.

These questions are referred to by some as the great "mysteries" of faith. It is true that philosophers and theologians have been offering their answers for a long time, though few of their intellectual arguments offer the comfort or courage that we, the everyday folks, need.

As we have already seen, however, there is One to whom we can turn when all reasoning fails—when there seem to be no answers at all. In the face of these deep mysteries, to which we now turn our attention, he does not stand somewhere above us, silent and serene, while we grapple in futility.

No, rather, our Savior comes to walk beside us, always, and all the way to our final victory.

11. A New Level of Maturity
Three Ways to Handle Uncertainty

From time to time, I encounter folks whose faith seems to rest on a rather simplistic assumption. I am referring to the people who say, "I don't have to worry, because God tells me exactly what I'm supposed to do all the time."

How wonderful it would be to have a direct, clear, and open pipeline to heaven twenty-four hours a day. Perhaps you, too, have met people who have God standing at their elbow, who are never wrong about the will of God, who never bump their forehead on a closed door.

IT IS NORMAL TO LIVE WITH SOME UNCERTAINTIES

Not long ago, a stranger came up to me at the end of our early worship service. He said, "Preacher, I started to interrupt your first service but decided I'd wait until the one at eleven o'clock." (I was glad for that!) "You see," he rushed on, "when I woke up this morning, God told me to get on a bus and come down here to First Methodist Church and preach. So I guess I'll be preaching for you at the second service."

I said, "Mister, you've got your wires crossed somewhere, because just this morning the Lord told me I was supposed to preach at *both* services!"

As you can imagine, that response did not set well with my eager friend. What is sad to me is that there are so many people who are looking for a "prophet" like this man to come along and direct their every step.

Just about the time I met this character, I received a long-distance phone call from a friend who was quite excited. He explained that a "prophet" had moved into the community and was getting hundreds of messages from God each week. People were allowing this seer to direct even very intimate aspects of their lives, without question.

Since that phone call, I've thought deeply about the need we all have for guidance. I wish it were as easy as it seemed to the man who presented himself to preach or to the "prophet" who was spewing out messages from God. I wish we had a celestial ticker tape machine with certain designated attendants to mind it. When a portion of the tape came out with your name on it, these folk would clip it off and slip it into a basket with your name on it. Then, on your way home from work, you could stop and pick up your guidance for the next day.

The story of the prophet Balaam told in the Old Testament book of Numbers (chapter 22) shows us the plight of a person who was "too sure." The Bible tells us that Balaam was at home one day when the representatives of Balak, a Moabite king, came to him with fees in their hands. Balak wanted to oppose the army of Israel. He had heard about the potency of Balaam's blessings and curses and wanted to enlist his services against God's people.

When Balaam heard what the men wanted, he responded, as would any good man of God, by saying, "I must first spend the night in prayer."

The next morning Balaam had an answer for the king's men. He announced, "The Lord has told me not to go with you. I cannot curse the people of Israel."

When Balak learned of his reply, he just sweetened the pot, so to speak. He sent a more impressive entourage and even finer gifts. It was enough to get Balaam to say, "Hmmm. Let me pray one more time and see if the Lord has something different to say." This time, he came back and said, "I think the Lord wants me to go after all."

The rest of the story is well known by students of the Bible. Balaam rode his faithful donkey toward Balak's palace, but the creature saw an angel with his sword drawn, blocking their path. When Balaam finally saw the angel, he fell down and prayed, "I have sinned, Oh Lord. I did not know that you were blocking my way." Balaam had been so *sure* he knew the will of God, but even his donkey knew better!

Here was Balaam, the most prominent prophet of his day, no flimflam holy man. Here was a prophet known through the area, not in just one nation, but several, as a man who was mighty. Here was a prophet who prayed all night long, thought he knew the will of God, and yet went out to face an angel blocking his way! Knowing the will of God, then, is not always simple, nor is it always easy. If a prophet of God can be so obtuse, so slow to learn, I believe that it is all right for an average Christian to confess some uncertainties and to live with them.

Life is full of complexities. Sometimes we simply do not know what to do. But that doesn't stop people from looking for strong voices to tell them what to do. And though many of us would bridle at this idea, we all, at one time or another, are troubled by the need for direction. We want God to tell us, somehow, whether we should go to that college, accept a certain job offer, move or stay put. Though the Bible is full of wisdom, it will never tell you, on page 863, whom you ought to marry, for instance. Yet the Bible *has* promised that God will lead us.

On the other hand, there are people for whom the very notion that we can have divine guidance is simply preposterous. They say, "I don't believe in all that stuff the church peddles anyway. It's simpler to admit that I'm just a biological accident, then I can give myself over to following my desires and impulses. I'll use animal cunning to satisfy all my biological urges and be guided by my wits—which is all we have in the final analysis. People who want someone else to tell them how to live are weak." These folks are convinced, so they say, that they are at peace without a God telling them what to do.

There is even a third response to the idea of divine guidance that is less negative but still denies God's personal interest or intervention in our lives. In my experience, this type of thinking is also widespread and is even rampant in the church. The folks who think this way camouflage their unbelief. They still have their name on a church roll, and they show up in the pews now and again. Once in a while, for the benefit of the children, they have prayers before a meal.

But the thought that God will actually say something to *them*, that he might have the power to give them so much as a quiet assurance in their soul that there is something he wants them to do—well, the notion is too remote. More likely, they don't have room for such an intrusion into their lives. And so they fall into the grip of a grim kind of determinism that says, "Whatever will be, will be—so don't worry about it." These people have also settled into a satisfied rut, more or less without God.

For a thinking, believing Christian, however, neither of these approaches to guidance is desirable. In the first place, we know that we are not biological accidents but that we were created by God. Second, we know that we have a *purposeful* God who has not cut himself off from his creation. For those of us who have come to know God, even in the slightest, it is unthinkable that he would create us and then stand by and watch while we helplessly muddle from one mess to another until death comes to end it all.

Now on the other hand, let me quickly point out an opposite danger. While we cannot assume that God doesn't care, neither can we assume that our pipeline to heaven never gets clogged up. I am speaking here about balance. On one side we have presumption; on the reverse side, unbelief.

Paul Tournier, the Christian doctor and counselor, wrote that when you talk about the will of God, you are talking about one of the greatest paradoxes of the Christian faith. He says, we need the counsel of God in order to do what he wants, yet even the most fervent believer can be confused regarding what to do in a given instance.

Over the centuries Christians have learned foundational principles about the way we come to mature decisions with God's guidance. God has provided three strong "pillars" that we can build into our lives. The more we learn to rely on these supports, the more calmness and assurance we will find in those times when life threatens to go out of control.

GOD SPEAKS THROUGH THE BIBLE

The first of these pillars is the Bible. God speaks to us primarily through the Bible. As Christians we believe this, and we need to follow up by cultivating a working knowledge of the wisdom in its pages.

But of late many people, from the scholar to the completely illiterate, have argued that the Bible, an ancient book, is irrelevant to modern men and women. They say that the "thinking" person or the person who is "strong" need not rely on the Scriptures as a "crutch." One suspects that there is in their lives more than a hint of what the Bible itself calls "rebellion."

A second view of the Bible, held by many, very good Christians, is that it is a book about God's special saints. These Christians accept the Bible but see it as a book that is remote from their everyday lives. The problem with this view is that when we elevate the men and women of the Bible too high, they become unreachable. We can never be like them, never reach their level of maturity precisely because we start out thinking they are far better than we are.

In my thinking, however, we must get close to the stories of Jacob, Joseph, and David, and to the early disciples of Jesus, before we are ready for Paul's theoretical statements in Romans or Ephesians. For the truth is, the Bible is made up of stories about ordinary men and women who had to grow and mature and make difficult choices just as we do. Their stories told in the Bible offer us excellent guidance as we reshape our uncertainty and go on to a new level of maturity.

THE WISDOM OF THE CHURCH AND BELIEVING FRIENDS

The second pillar is the cumulative wisdom of the Church and of our believing friends. We can rely on them as we grow in the ability to make mature choices.

Just as there are many who are down on the Bible, the community of Christians has always had its antagonists. We commonly hear that the Church "is full of hypocrites." Still others latch onto one or two small doctrines and, when others don't agree with them, they pull away into tiny splinter groups. I am sorry for these folks.

When it comes to the accumulation of shared experiences, who can measure the wisdom of the community of faith? Who can replace what we have learned in the commonality of our struggles? We can never forget that, through the Church, that collection of men and women who were as imperfect as we are, God produced the New Testament.

I would go so far as to say that it is *only* as we interact with other Christians that we come to the place where we can make mature decisions regarding ourselves and others. With the exception of those who are physically unable to attend church, no Christian can rely solely on a televised gospel message. The isolated Christian is a contradiction in terms. There is a wealth of wisdom and caring concern in our churches, Sunday schools, and in home prayer groups. We are cheating ourselves if we do not draw upon these resources.

It is only as we interact with other Christians that we come to the place where we can make mature decisions regarding ourselves and others.

The most well-meaning, God-fearing person who shuns the wisdom and counsel of others because he has "heard a voice" is always going to be on unsteady ground. Through others, God's inspirations are confirmed. And through others, we sometimes find that we are not yet on the mark. To avoid or discount the voice of flesh-and-blood men and women is a sign, not of maturity, but of the one who is headed backward toward an infantile insistence on having his own way.

THE STILL, SMALL VOICE

Now, as strongly as I have made this one point, we cannot deny the third pillar that upholds us when we have to make choices. That is, God *can* speak to us inwardly by means of that "still, small voice."

There are times when we are suddenly struck with an idea that rings like a bell in the depths of our soul. In those moments, we are overwhelmed by a sense of "knowing" what is the right decision. Perhaps we are still at the stage in our spiritual growth that we are not sure of the source of this knowing—but it is from God.

I know a man named Julian Hutchison, a deeply sincere man and a loving father. Julian's son told him he was going hunting on the morning of his eighteenth birthday. That morning was the last time he saw his son alive. Later in the day, the terrible news came. The boy had been killed accidentally.

For weeks and weeks, Julian was nearly beside himself with grief. One Sunday, after a communion service at church, he continued to kneel alone at the altar rail, nearly swallowed up by his inner pain.

Suddenly, Julian felt a hand on his shoulder—but there was no one there! And then he heard in his heart the words, "It's all right. Your son is with me."

There are times when we are suddenly struck with an idea that rings like a bell in the depths of our soul. In those moments, we are overwhelmed by a sense of "knowing" what is the right decision.

Though Julian's pain at the loss of his son did not vanish overnight, he will never lose the comfort that came in that moment of "knowing" that his son is with the Lord.

There is another type of "knowing": those moments when we feel God is revealing his directions, such as the illuminated experience that I discussed in chapter 2 when I knew I was called to the ministry.

Quite often, when we examine these bursts of guidance, we find that they are not altogether outside the context of past experiences. The truth of the matter is, God may plant an idea in our hearts early, even in a rudimentary form, only to highlight it later in one of those bell-ringing experiences that we call unusual.

This is when the community of Christians can provide wisdom and support. For as we share our thoughts and plans with others, we may find that they are not so "unusual" after all. Other Christians can support us by praying and listening to God on our behalf and by sharing guidance from the Scriptures. They can give valuable words of caution, advice. They can offer the kind of thumbs-up approval that helps us overcome doubt and fear and make decisions with boldness. In the case of my conversion and call to the ministry, supportive confirmation came from my mother and other Christians who were close to me.

And so what emerges is a balanced picture. We have three bastions of stability to support us: the Word of God, the wisdom of the Church, and the inner leading of the Holy Spirit. When we emphasize one over the others, we do not stand on solid footing, for they were meant to work together.

WALKING IN DARKNESS, TRUSTING IN GOD

I must add another word to this matter of guidance and choice. Because we are moving "toward maturity" it is still probable that we will make wrong moves.

After I had been in the ministry for some years and was pastor of a local church, I was planning a very definite career change for myself that involved becoming a teacher. I thought I was supposed to go to a certain seminary and become a professor. Every time the number of candidates for the job was narrowed down, I was still in the running. Then only two of us were left vying for the seminary job. I practically had my bags packed.

And then, as far as I was concerned, disaster struck. When it came down to the final choice for the position, the other candidate was selected. I'd been so sure! Now I was crestfallen. Suddenly, my future stretched before me uncertainly. For some time I mourned that change of course.

Subsequent events, however, showed that disappointment to be one of the greatest days of my life. Groping through that dead end renewed and deepened my contact with the living God. I became more sensitive toward people who struggle with the uncertainties of life. Because of that time of reevaluation, I discovered opportunities to serve God in new and entirely different ways.

I came to a more mature outlook on life and to a stronger position in my faith. For the greatest comfort comes from knowing that, even when we're moving with the best light we have, that light may not be good enough. But we need not fear, for our lives are in the hands of One who is far greater. We can commit our steps to an all-knowing, all-seeing God and be assured that "he will make straight your paths" (Proverbs 3:6).

It's comforting to know that a real warrior of the faith like the Apostle Paul also met with uncertainty at crucial moments in his life. From his experience, we can gain deeper insights.

In Acts chapter 16, we read that Paul was on his second missionary journey. The Holy Spirit had set him apart for this mission, and the whole church was praying for him. We know that Paul was not one to flip a coin about which way he should go; he steeped his decisions in prayer. As far as he knew, he was going to travel throughout Asia Minor to spread the good news about Jesus Christ. He had passed through the southern provinces, establishing churches, until he came to the borders of one of the northernmost provinces, Bithynia. He was all set to enter this province, but the Spirit would not allow him to enter.

Paul was acting in good faith, according to what he thought God wanted him to do. Yet he was blocked, frustrated by God. He thought he was on the right track, but he was not. Paul may even have gotten sick, because at this point Luke, the physician, joined him. We know for sure that, at this moment, when the way seemed closed, something exciting and new happened: Paul received the call to carry the gospel beyond the Middle East and Asia into Europe. This was a faith adventure, something no one else had ever done.

But let's not forget that small slice of time when Paul had no inkling of what God was up to. I believe it was *that* moment, and many others like it in Paul's experience, that prompted him to say life is like baffling reflections in a mirror. He affirmed that, while we cannot see the way clearly now, one day we will see all things clearly (see 1 Corinthians 13).

You see, when it comes to growing in maturity, part of the process is the ability to walk into darkness, holding God's hand in the midst of uncertainty. Maturing involves trusting that God will guide us, even when we're not sure of the right way to go. He means to work with us in shaping our destiny, opening new doors we never could have imagined.

For the God we serve will always guide and mold us lovingly, even in those times when a donkey can see something we can't see. And I, for one, will always be glad about that!

12. Walking on Wounded Feet

The Companion Beside Us in Suffering

One September night, following a minor surgery in which the surgeon performed a biopsy on Jean, I took her into my arms. I had to tell this beautiful woman I love so much, my bride since she was nineteen, that the biopsy was positive.

"There is a malignancy," I said, my voice trembling, "and we'll have to go with radical surgery."

Following Jean's surgery, the memory that stands out most vividly is our first visit to the oncologist's office for a follow-up examination. It was one of the most over-full offices I have ever seen. Every seat was taken.

I thought, as I looked at all the faces, "We each have the same story. We're at different places, and the details may vary. But we're on the same road—and the road is crowded."

Nobody in that waiting room said very much. Their eyes told their story, however, and they asked a question. That story is *my* story, and Jean's, for we felt a oneness with each person there.

Behind every human suffering, emotional or physical, lies the question: why is there suffering at all?

WHY IS THERE SUFFERING?

Sometimes we think that we in the twentieth century are the most clever and insightful people of all time. But when we ask about the "why" of suffering, we are really joining our voices to countless others down through all the ages who have witnessed pain and wondered.

The problem of suffering was certainly around in Jesus' day. Perhaps, having the Master of all creation in their midst, the disciples thought they would get a clear answer and solve that mystery once and for all. Let's look at an encounter in which they had the perfect opportunity to pose their question.

In John chapter 9, we read that Jesus was on his way out of Jerusalem, having taught in the temple. The disciples were with him, and there along the road was a blind man. Evidently the disciples knew him, because they were aware that he was blind from birth. Now Jesus had just conversed with the Pharisees, and in that debate he claimed that he and God the Father were one. So when the disciples saw this blind man, groping his way along the road, they decided to get some answers to an ever-troubling dilemma.

Behind every human suffering, emotional or physical, lies the question: why is there suffering at all?

The disciples asked Jesus, "Lord, tell us something. Why was this man born blind? Was it his sin or the sin of his parents that caused his suffering?"

You see, at that time, many believed there was a causal relationship between sin and sickness. If you sinned, God would afflict you. They also thought the reverse was true: if you were sick or something bad happened to you, then it stood to reason that you had sinned. There were even some who taught that a child could sin while in the mother's womb, and this teaching may also have been at the root of the disciples' question.

In fact, the same unfortunate, cause-effect thinking about sin and sickness is still alive today—and this despite the fact that Jesus' immediate response challenged the faulty suppositions.

Jesus replied, "Neither this man nor his parents have sinned."

In this he was saying, "Sometimes we suffer because we live in a fallen, imperfect world." Period. Then, without any more explanation than that, Jesus performed a miracle and healed that blind man.

Would that God always came through with a miracle! We know, of course, that not all suffering finds its answer in a quick and easy miracle. Therefore, we must look deeper into Jesus' true observation about our fallen world.

Any discussion of human suffering must take into account human ignorance. There are many things that we do willingly, not knowing they are detrimental to us in the long run. In this, I think about my father.

Twenty-five years ago my father died suddenly of a heart attack. For a long time, I raised all kinds of questions: why should such a good man die so young? Why couldn't he have lived to see and enjoy his grandchildren? But as time passed, I began to look back and discover some causes.

To begin with, my father was quite overweight. Add to that the fact that he smoked too much. Long after his death, I also read a list of foods that we are supposed to avoid because they are high in cholesterol and triglycerides. Too much of these substances is bad for your arteries and heart, but that fact wasn't widely known twenty-five years ago. When I compared the list with my father's diet, I realized that ninety-five percent of what he ate was slowly killing him. And we just didn't know.

I also think about thalidomide, a drug that used to be given to help women who were experiencing difficult pregnancies. Though it helped the mothers, the drug also caused many children to be born with physical deformities and handicaps. And then there are the problems that have come from asbestos, which was used to insulate buildings, and Agent Orange, which was used to defoliate the jungles of Vietnam. Only after it was too late and many lives were harmed did we learn the harmful effects of these substances.

You can multiply these examples many times, and what you come up with is simple human ignorance. You can hear Jesus praying, "Oh Father, help them. They don't know what they are doing to themselves and to their children."

Then again, there are those sufferings that we bring upon ourselves through making choices we know are wrong. Any discussion of suffering must also acknowledge that we have freedom of
choice.

The other day, for instance, I was in an airport waiting area
when I noticed a young couple. The woman was pregnant. I
thought, "What a happy time for them." Then I noticed something that distressed me greatly. The woman had a cigarette in
one hand and a cocktail in the other. As soon as she finished
smoking one cigarette, she lit up another. And the moment her
glass was empty, she was back at the bar getting a second drink,
and a third, and a fourth.

The news media bombard us constantly with scientific facts
proving that every time an expectant mother drinks alcohol or
smokes tobacco, she is delivering a chemical sledge-hammer blow
to her unborn child. It has long been known that nicotine and
alcohol can travel through the placenta, adversely affecting an
infant in the womb. And recently, it was reported that a woman
who drinks alcohol doubles her chances of having breast cancer.
Such knowledge is no secret today.

Yet many insist on ignoring the danger signals. I have to con-
clude that the woman who persists in smoking and drinking when
she knows the dangers, must forfeit her right to stand over the
crib of a less-than-perfect child and blame God.

If we know what is right and choose to do wrong, we cannot
demand that God save us from the results of our own choices.
He may respond to our prayers, because he is loving and full of
mercy—but if we refuse to play by the rules he has revealed to
us we have no *right* to question or demand of him. We forfeit the
right to ask, "Why?"

Throughout the Bible, God placed clear choices before us. The
Old Testament in particular is full of instances in which God said,
"Do *this,* and you will live." Likewise, in John 3:19 Jesus said,
"And this is the judgment, that the light has come into the world,
and men loved darkness rather than light, because their deeds
were evil." And though some of Jesus' disciples recognized that
he alone held "the words of life," many turned from him, just as
many continue to do today.

We learn from Scripture that God has created a moral, orderly
universe. When we break his law, we can expect to suffer painful

consequences. In Paul's words, "Whatever a man sows, that he will also reap" (Galatians 6:7). You cannot go against the grain of the universe and complain because it gives you splinters.

But all this leaves us with the old theory: "When you sin, bad things will happen to you." There is yet another reality implied in Jesus' observation about our fallen world. We suffer sometimes because there is a power of evil at work in the world.

At some time in his ministry, every pastor will stand at a certain graveside and feel nearly helpless. There are those gut-wrenching experiences when we have to find, from somewhere, the words and the courage to comfort. Perhaps it is the grieving young widow whose husband succumbed to cancer, leaving her with small children; perhaps it is the parents of a tiny child killed in a tragic accident.

How painfully I recall one of the worst tragedies I have faced as a pastor.

There was a lovely Christian woman in a church I once served in Columbus, Georgia. She sang in the choir at both services every Sunday morning. She had been active in Sunday School for so many years that there was a class named for her and her late husband. Her two sons also attended the church, largely because she had prayed each of them into a personal relationship with Jesus Christ. Each Sunday, just before I stepped up to the pulpit, this dear woman would hug me and whisper, "I'm praying for you." She put a spring in the step of everyone she met.

In and around the Columbus area, there was another noted individual—noted, that is, for evil. For seven years, police hunted for a man known only as "the Columbus strangler," who brutally murdered six women, spreading fear throughout the area. I had no idea, every Sunday morning, that I was being prayed for by his seventh and final victim.

I will never forget the shock and numbness on the morning of her funeral, nor the faces of her sons as they sat there in the front row. Suffering was etched on every face.

GOD LOVES HIS CHILDREN

At moments like that we feel woefully inadequate in our attempt to bring comfort. Yet there *is* a comfort we can and *must* offer to the hurting. It begins with this: we know what God the

Father is like because we have looked into the face of Jesus Christ. From what we see in Jesus' life, we know that God does not deal unfairly with his children, maliciously doling out suffering. God does not send sickness or disease or death upon anyone.

How do we know that? First, because Jesus said he had come "to plunder Satan's domain." Evil and sickness and death belong to the wicked one. Jesus, on the other hand, spent his ministry healing people wherever he went. So it makes no sense to blame God for tragedy. Why would God be working against himself?

Second, we see in Jesus a great depth of compassion. He is not untouched by our pain. He wept at the death of his friend Lazarus; his heart was broken by the grief of the widow who had lost her son. This is the compassion that we rely on in our dark hour.

Still the mystery remains for many: "Why does God *allow* tragedy and suffering?"

When it comes to this eternal question, every one of us must be honest. We shake our heads, even in the midst of our faith, and admit, "I don't know why." When we live in a fallen world like ours, we and those we love are likely to suffer at some time. Just as we peer into the face of Jesus and know that God is fair, we can also look into the faces of others who suffer and open ourselves to the most profound lessons of faith written there.

When I think of my friend, Fran King, I am reminded that God is able to do more than we could ask or hope or think.

Fran, who was a member of a church I served, discovered that she had a terminal illness. Together, we struggled through all the stages of her grief, and finally she came to an acceptance of the fact that she was not going to live much longer in this world.

One day, in October of that year, she came and asked me to pray a special prayer with her. Hers was a close family, including five children. The three girls had all been in local beauty contests, and the two sons, stars on their football team, were also very handsome. It was wonderful to see them together. And so, I readily agreed when Fran asked, "Pray that God will let me live so we can be together for one more Christmas."

Just at Thanksgiving, however, she took a turn for the worse. A few days after, she died. I, and others who knew the prayer of her heart, could not help but wonder why God had denied such a simple request. For days I was greatly troubled.

It was not until I began to work on her funeral sermon that I was given the insight. I wanted to leap up and run, to clap my hands and shout. I couldn't wait to share my insight with the family. I wanted to say to them, "God didn't give Fran Christmas like she asked; he gave her Easter instead!"

That's the way it is with our God. We ask for one thing, and he comes to us bearing a matchless gift that is far better.

And there is another dear friend whose suffering was of a different sort. In him, I saw an incomparable heroism.

It was a Saturday morning some years ago, and the insistent ring of the telephone would not let me sleep late. The voice on the other end of the line was that of a friend who had recently become a Christian. He was desperate, he said, to talk with me.

We met for breakfast at a nearby restaurant and, the moment I sat down at the table, he poured out his problem. He was in a construction-related business and, in the past, he had collaborated with several other firms in that city in rigging their bids. They were scheduled to have another meeting about an upcoming bid, and my friend's new convictions as a Christian loomed before him.

His dilemma was no small matter. If he withdrew from the price-fixing ring, he would suddenly find himself in direct, affrontive competition. There was no question the others would band together then to put him out of business. And he could not go to the authorities because he was deeply implicated by his previous involvement with the group.

The decision was not an easy one, but he chose to withdraw from the unethical activity. The consequences were severe. Time after time, he was underbid by one of his former friends. His business and his family suffered greatly because of the drastic reduction in income.

I was with this brave friend years later on the night before he died. He had paid an awful price, in many ways, for his commitment to Christ, but in his heart he was in perfect peace. He died with the joy of knowing that God had given him the courage to do the right thing.

Yes, we must also come to grips with the fact that sometimes we will suffer because we are trying to do the right thing in a crooked world. Throughout the New Testament, we are not told that the way before us, that straight and narrow road, will be easy.

THE PROMISE OF ETERNITY

Despite these penetrating lessons, we still recognize that none of these good folks—not Fran King, or my friend in construction—ever received a complete answer regarding their sufferings.

Millions have admired that marvelous old saint, Corrie ten Boom, who suffered in a Nazi concentration camp because she and her family helped Jews who were escaping Europe. Corrie loved to quote the verse:

> Not till the looms are silent
> and the shuttles cease to fly
> shall God unroll the canvas
> and reveal the reason why.

On one level, we have to settle for that until the day of revealing. And this causes us to take into account another aspect of reality: heaven.

To talk about human, earthly suffering and not consider the promise of heaven is to leave off the most important dimension. Deuteronomy 33:27 promises, "The eternal God is your dwelling place, and underneath are the everlasting arms."

It was our Lord, Jesus, who came to make real those everlasting arms, which give the hope and promise of eternity with God. Because Jesus knew about the reality of heaven, he could be remarkably and creatively careless with the lives of his disciples.

He said to them, "Look, I'm sending you out into the world. And I want you to know it's dangerous out there. You're going to have tribulation. Men are going to be like ravenous wolves tearing you apart. But don't worry about the suffering and injustice of it all. I'll make it right in the next world, where your names are written in the Book of Life. Things will be as they ought to be."

Behind every promise Jesus made, lies the question, "Do you have the faith to believe what I am telling you is true—to look beyond the present reality and trust me?" He is still asking that question of us today.

Do you believe that earth has no sorrow that heaven cannot heal? Do you believe that Jesus is on the side of right? Do you know that he cares—that he bears the pain of your heart when you've said goodbye to the one who is dearest to you? Can you answer, "Oh, yes. He cares. I know he cares. His heart is touched with my grief."?

One member of our church in Houston shared a beautiful story with me just the other day. When her firstborn child, a son, came into the world, he brought with him one of those great big mysteries. The doctors recognized at once that the tiny infant was born with an imperfectly formed heart. Even before she took the child home from the hospital, they were making preparations for surgery.

The Companion who walks beside us, understanding every sorrow and counting every tear, walks on wounded feet.

Slow years passed. One medical procedure followed another. Always those parents held onto the hope that maybe *this* procedure would solve their son's problem. They held on despite the fact that the doctors did not give them much hope. Finally, the little boy died.

The mother was greatly tested. She couldn't sleep. She agonized. She prayed. After a time, in the middle of one of those long, solitary sessions of prayer, she told me it was as though she could hear a voice deep in her soul. She recognized it as the voice of Jesus, and he was speaking to her about her son.

He said to her, "Everything is as it ought to be." That was all. And yet, with that eternal perspective, with that promise, she was filled with peace. She found the joy of living once more.

Do you trust him like that? Even when you cannot find the reason "why," do you know the support and security of God's everlasting arms? If you need this surety, this comfort, then give your life fully to him. Open your heart to him. Give him your suffering and your questions.

For this one thing I know. The Companion who walks beside us, understanding every sorrow and counting every tear, walks on wounded feet.

13. God Knows What He Is Doing

Coming Out on Top (When You Think You're at the Bottom)

The Apostle Paul was one who made some astounding claims. One that has challenged many people is this one from his letter to the Romans:

> We know that in everything God works for good with those who love him, who are called according to his purpose. . . . Who shall separate us from the love of Christ?
>
> (Romans 8:28, 35)

*Every*thing? Can we really believe such a claim?

Several years ago I watched a drama unveil in the life of a family that was deeply committed to the church.

The father was a teacher in a local high school and his wife played the piano in church. They had a growing son who was looking toward college and, like most families in that position, they were facing an economic crunch. They had accumulated only a small savings account. The house in which they lived was on the way to being paid for, but all in all their estate was not very large. They didn't see how they could cover the high cost of a college education.

Increasingly, the husband felt the need to go into business on his own. The venture he wanted to launch required their total life savings, plus remortgaging their home to the hilt. It meant risking everything. They didn't rush into the decision, but called on their pastors and people in their Sunday School class, asking us to pray. We did. He had skill, a college degree, and a grand personality. But what we prayed was for God to lead this man and woman and give them his peace. They especially wanted to know that this business was not only a sound investment but also was really God's will for them. Finally, after financial calculations and months of agonizing, the husband quit his teaching job and they launched out in business on their own.

From the outset we all watched, heartsick, as the business steadily plummeted downhill. It happened to be one of those ill-fated times when the bottom fell out in that particular field. Before long, they were out of business. They lost all that they'd invested—their savings, their home. The man couldn't even get back into his teaching position. This lovely, faithful couple were forced at last to move from the church and community they loved in search of a job somewhere else.

Today, they are slowly remaking their lives. And many who watched from the sidelines, myself included, have been forced to ask: are all things working together for *good* in the lives of these people who loved and sought God? Didn't God know what he was doing when he allowed that praying couple to get into that particular business at that particular time? With so many of us praying sincerely for them, it would seem that God could have nudged even *one* of us with a cautionary note. What good purpose could he possibly bring out of this disaster?

In the face of such a mystery as that, a question flies at us right out of the Scriptures: "How can we know—when we've sought his guidance and life comes tumbling in around us—that God is working for our good?" Or are we crazy, deluding ourselves to think that?

GOD KNOWS WHAT IS BEST FOR HIS CHILDREN

Of course, answers to such questions can only come to those who are first willing to reach out beyond the physical circumstances and make several basic affirmations. First among them is this: God knows what is best for his children.

There are many among us, philosophers and common people alike, who would say that foundational statement requires too great a leap of faith. Does it?

You and I are creatures of the hour. We cannot see into the future. We do not always recognize what is best for us. Sometimes we believe we *must* have a certain thing. Subsequent years may reveal, however, that the very thing we demanded was exactly what we should *not* have had.

Who among us, as a parent, has not seized a shiny knife or a bottle of poisonous household cleanser from the hands of a curious little child? Explaining that the child cannot have the desired object because it is dangerous does no good either. All you get sometimes is a temper tantrum. But of course a wise parent ignores the tears and screaming, knowing that the child must be kept from bodily injury, perhaps even death.

I'm reminded of just how shortsighted I am when I think of the advice I gave my daughter Elizabeth as she left home for college. In her last year of high school, while we were living on the East Coast, she announced that her heart was set on attending Rice University in Houston. I had one big question for her: "Why in the world are you going way out there? She, however, for some unknown reason, settled on that school and *had* to go there.

Well, I summoned all my fatherly wisdom and, just before she left, laid it on her. I said, "Okay, we've agreed to send you to Rice. But above all, do not go out West and fall in love with one of those cowboys. Don't marry anybody who's going to settle west of the Mississippi. Make sure they live in the East—or we'll never get to see our grandchildren."

She did exactly what her father told her to do. A few years later, she fell in love with a young man from Virginia. And now— since I received a call to a pulpit in Houston—we pass like ships in the night: We went West, and our daughter went East!

I'm not going to evade the first issue—whether God is really working on our behalf—by glibly saying what's bad turns out to be good. That isn't always the case. There is nothing in the Bible or elsewhere in the universe that says bad things automatically turn out right for the good person. Not at all. The church today has run the gamut with such superficial theology.

I was walking through a shopping mall a few months ago, when a display in a bookstore window caught my eye. Propped on the display was a copy of the book being featured, and above it was a sign: "Answers." Apparently, the book hadn't sold too well at its cover price, because the bookstore managers had written in a sale price in bright red marker. As I got closer, I saw that they'd even cut the sale price.

I had to chuckle as I thought, "Yessir, answers are getting cheaper all the time." Many of us want to come up with quick and easy answers to everything.

However! There is a big however at loose in the universe. A surprising number of the things we think are terrible turn out in the long run to be pretty good. Jean and I discovered that when we came to the end of our first four-year appointment in the Methodist Church.

We'd been pastoring a congregation of wonderful people. But, like most young men, I was looking forward to moving up the ladder. At the end of four years, we were promised a church in a county-seat town. It wasn't much of a town, only three thousand people. But to be the pastor of a county-seat church when you're in your mid-twenties and slowly starving to death is really exciting.

And there was more sweetener in the pot. The new church was also excited about our coming. Even before the appointment was firm, I learned that they were going to raise our salary. More than that, they were renovating the parsonage, putting in air-conditioning—that was really something in those days—and a dishwasher. They'd even painted the kitchen a nice, warm yellow. Emotionally, we'd already moved into that air-conditioned parsonage with the yellow kitchen. Our prayer every night was very simple: "Oh Lord, don't let the bishop and the cabinet gum it up!"

Feverishly, we packed. Then, the Friday before we were to move, we got the news: somebody else was going to get our yellow kitchen! We were being assigned to a little old church down on the coast where the sand gnats buzzed right through the screens at night and ate people alive while they slept. Its parsonage didn't even have a fan. And then we found out it was also *less* pay.

I cried out to God, "I told you I was your man. Now you're supposed to take care of me. How on earth could you let something like this happen to me and my family—and to my career?" I thought, in my mid-twenties, I was at the end of my career. Instead of going up, I was going down.

We moved to the coast anyway—grudgingly, I must admit. How was I to know at the start that that little congregation would explode in growth, that they would build not only a new educational building, but a new parsonage as well? And those were just the superficial blessings. How was I to know that, after two years there, the church people would give to me a sacrificial gift that will last a lifetime? One day, over a surprise lunch, I was told, "We're going to increase your salary and send you back to school for three years to earn your doctorate. We'll run the church during the week and you can come home to preach on weekends."

And when we'd lost our yellow kitchen, we thought life was going to be downhill from there.

The first question we need to ask then is not about God's willingness to work on our behalf, but, "Who are we to think we know what's best in the long run?"

GOD WANTS THE BEST FOR HIS CHILDREN

Reflecting on that first question leads us to another of those leap-of-faith affirmations: God not only *knows* what's best for his children, he also *wants* the best for us. Because of my inability to see into tomorrow I am thankful that my destiny is not in my own imperfect hands but rests in his.

This gives a huge problem to those who have bought the lie that we human beings are the shapers of our own destiny.

That does not mean that we Christians stumble through life never taking any responsibility and never making any decisions. It doesn't mean that at all. Like our friends whose business went sour, we make decisions just like every other person. We bathe those decisions in prayer. We lean on the Word of God. We turn to our Christian friends for counsel. And after we get all the light available to us, in fear and trembling, we make our move. We step out.

But we know that the only understanding of God's will that even approaches an accurate perspective is what we see when we look back. Only then can we begin to understand the perfect will of God. And though we make our decisions with fear and trembling, there is one chief difference: we Christians believe we do not blunder our way from one irredeemable disaster to another.

Rather, our confidence is in a God who, if we let him, will engineer our circumstances and will bring us out where we ought to come out. We know that he is working within a process to bring good, even to redeem awful situations.

God not only knows *what is best for his children, he also* wants *the best for us.*

Therefore we do not become bitter because of our mistakes. We do not become hardened or get down on ourselves and stay depressed. Instead, we understand that this God is in there with us, saying "yes" to us. And what we must do is say "yes" to him! Surely mistakes and suffering are woven into the fabric of life, but Paul says every hardship can be a prelude to glory!

God has given us the Holy Spirit as his guarantee of the good things to come (Ephesians 1:13–14). Imagine! God has given us himself, if you please, as a down payment on his own promise. Romans 8 tells us he even prays for us when we cannot pray aright for ourselves. The whole Godhead is on our side. Once you come to the realization that your life is in bigger hands than yours, then you will know for sure that our God can be trusted.

ARE YOU SURE ABOUT GOD?

Some things we just need to know *for sure.* The Apostle Paul, in Romans 8:28, did not say, "I believe God is at work." He didn't say, "in my opinion," or "I think." He said, "We *know* that in all things God works for the good. . . ."

Somebody asked Robert Browning, "What is the one theme in all your poetry most representative of you and who you are?" Browning readily replied, "I am very sure about God."

Are you very sure about God? That he is a wise parent who loves you?

I have a good friend who is a pastor of the First Methodist Church in Tulsa. His name is Jimmy Buskirk. Not long after he went into the ministry, Jimmy was stricken with what was believed to be an incurable eye disease. One day, his father went with him to the eye specialist and was with Jimmy when he heard the frightening news. The doctor told him, "Unless you get a transplant we cannot save your vision."

A few minutes later, Jimmy and his dad were alone. His father gently laid a hand on his shoulder and said, "Son, I've lived most of my life. You're on the threshold of a great career in ministry, a great calling. You need to be equipped with good vision. I want to give you my eyes."

As it turned out, Jimmy didn't have to consider that wonderful offer for very long. Miraculously, he was healed. But Jimmy told me much later, "That night when we got home from the doctor's office, I wept like a baby. Not just with the realization that my daddy was willing to give his eyes to me, but because I kept remembering what Jesus said: 'If you who are evil know how to give good gifts to your children—just think how much more God wants to give good gifts to you!'" He said, "I was literally overwhelmed by the love of God flooding into my soul with its sureness."

Maybe you need to be sure about God in your life. Maybe when that assurance comes, you can stand up to the worst in life and be convinced that the God who holds you in his hands is the all-wise, all-knowing, all-loving Father.

I remember reading a story in the *Evangel* magazine about the final days of Frances Havergal, the great hymn writer. She, who had loved God all her life, was in her eighties. Coming to the last day of her life, she was with a friend, who read these words to her from Isaiah: "I the Lord have called thee in righteousness, and will hold thine hand, and will keep thee" (Isaiah 42:6).

Frances Havergal stopped the woman and said, "Did you hear that? We are called, we are held, and we are kept. I believe I can go home on that." And she did.

No matter what's happening in our lives, we have the assurance that we are *called, held,* and *kept* in the hand of our heavenly Father.

I believe that Frances Havergal had that knowledge through much of her life. Her great faith inspired her to write such moving words as these:

> Hidden in the hollow of His blessed hand,
> Never foe can follow, never traitor stand;
> Not a surge of worry, not a shade of care,
> Not a blast of hurry touch the spirit there.
>
> Stayed upon Jehovah, hearts are fully blest,
> Finding, as He promised, perfect peace and rest!

With an assurance like that in my heart, I can lift my head, ready for the greatest transformation of all —the journey toward home.

14. The Home Field Advantage
The Final Reshaping

Every sports enthusiast knows that when a team plays on its home field it has a distinct advantage. Something about the familiarity of the setting and the electricity of the hometown crowd combine to give a team confidence, no matter how tough the opponent. Even professional analysts have learned to figure in this immeasurable but definite factor when trying to determine which team is favored to win.

Long before sports writers discovered the home field advantage, however, the writers of the Bible knew that factor was an important one for the Christian. Paul, for example, liked to compare life to a great race. In Hebrews 12:1, we are reminded that, as we run toward our goal, "we are surrounded by so great a cloud of witnesses." Therefore, we are strengthened to "run with perseverance the race marked out for us."

In other words, we have the advantage of having a great, heavenly crowd of spectators cheering us on to victory. When you know that someone important is watching, it's always a rousing source of inspiration, isn't it? It can reshape a defeated, beaten-down spirit into one that is fueled by determination.

WE ARE PART OF A GREAT FAMILY

Elton Trueblood, the contemporary Christian philosopher, believes we lost something very important when we decided to separate the church from the cemetery. Some of us grew up during a time when "God's little acre" was right beside or behind the church. You never went to church without seeing those silent, stone sentinels pointing upward toward the life beyond. Trueblood says that it's as natural for someone to be buried from the church as it is to carry a letter to the post office.

Today, oddly enough, many Christians don't want to think about death—it seems so "negative." To them, as to the rest of the folks in our culture, only the present moment is important. We no longer take to heart David's words when he wrote, "For I am thy passing guest, a sojourner, like all my fathers" (Psalm 39:12). We want to build our mansions, forgetting that we really live in tents. What is it that we have lost?

Trueblood believes that when we connect birth, life, and death—those great mysteries that the church celebrates—it creates within us a sense of eternity. When we lose that connection, we lose a sense of the continuity. We lose the sense that we are part of a vast family containing all those who have gone before us and all who will come after, greater than anything we can know here on earth. Paul, in writing Hebrews, wanted to drive home that sense of continuity. And so he called to mind the image of countless "witnesses," a vast crowd of those who have given a good testimony.

Immediately, you and I can call to mind faces both imagined and familiar: the faces of Moses, Peter, and the other apostles, the face of a departed grandmother whose prayers made all the difference in our life. We, like players on a field, consider those who have gone before, drawing strength from their support.

Historians have written that, on the night before a great battle, Napoleon's commanders all went to their commander's tent one by one. Reportedly, it was a strange procession, for no one said a word as they came into Napoleon's presence. Each man looked into his eyes, shook his hand, turned and walked out of the tent ready to lay down his life for his beloved general. What quality of strength and confidence and assurance was there in his face that, without speaking a word, he could impart such courage to other men?

In the midst of those lovely faces that we can call to mind, we also see one looming larger than the rest—the face of Jesus Christ. Paul's words ring with exultation as he reminds us to fix our eyes upon Jesus, seated on high. He is our goal, the author and perfecter of our faith.

WHO IS THE SHAPER OF YOUR FAITH?

Now stop right there a moment. *Who* is the author of your faith? Is it Jesus? Truly? This is not a theological question, but one that each of us must resolve daily as we run our race. Because if we don't have that issue settled at the center of our being as we begin, then we won't have *conviction* in our arsenal of weapons when evil besets us on the way. We are not ready to live this life fully, freely, or happily until we have in hand our passport to the world to come. Let me illustrate.

Some years ago, I was preparing to lead a tour to the Holy Land. It was Sunday, late, and I had preached three times that day. That evening, I hurried home to pack because we were to leave early the next morning. I had finished folding clothes into my suitcase, then went to open the little green file box where we kept important papers—including my passport.

The passport was not there. I flipped through the papers several times. Nothing.

Now I never panic in situations like that. Some people do. Instead, I call Jean. I'm the world's greatest loser of things, and she's the world's best finder. She will even tell me right where to look, and I tell her I've already looked there. Then she comes over and puts her hand on the lost article, right where she said it would be. If she can't find what I've lost, then I panic.

She could not find my passport.

For a couple of hours, we turned the house upside-down. Upstairs we could hear the excited voices of some relatives who were spending the night because they were going on the tour—the one that I would *not* be leading if we did not find that passport.

At midnight, I went to my church office and dumped all my files out on the floor. At 3:30 A.M. I called the travel agent, who assured me there was nothing he could do and hung up. About four in the morning, I went back home, praying fervently all the way. (If I prayed like that all the time, I'd be a better man!)

When I got home, I took a look at that green box and said, "Lord, I've *got* to have that passport." I reached back into the box and happened to pick up a plastic sleeve that held an insurance policy. I shook it. Out fell the passport.

I went to bed—at least part of me did. My heels and the back of my head touched the mattress. But I just lay there stiff as a board, thinking about how I had almost missed getting into the Promised Land because I didn't have the right credentials.

The point is this: we all need to be certain that we have in hand the right credentials that will open the way for us to pass peacefully from this world to the next.

That passport is faith in Jesus Christ. It is the reason we feel sorry for some of the wealthiest, most powerful men in history, while we rejoice for the lowliest Christian.

Once, on another trip to the Middle East, I visited the antiquities museum in Cairo where I saw all the treasures that once belonged to the great pharaoh we know as King Tut. I was awed to see that it took several halls the size of gymnasiums to contain the gold, silver, and jeweled treasures that were buried with that man, not the least of which was a 240-pound casket of pure gold. The only hope those ancient priests could offer their people was that Tut might carry these gifts into the afterlife with him and, perhaps, appease the fierce anger of the Egyptian gods of death. It was all chancy, and their gods were full of unpredictably dark whims.

From there I traveled directly to the biblical city of Thyatira in what is now Turkey. I went to see the old, ruined church where the early Christians worshiped. To follow Jesus in that era was to sentence yourself to become the poorest of the poor, because Christians were not allowed to sell their goods in the marketplace.

As I walked through those dusty ruins, pieces of broken pottery littered the rubble. I asked the guide what they represented. He said, "Those are pieces of burial pots. The people wanted to be buried in their church, beneath the floor, close to the altar."

Suddenly, that rubble became for me holy ground, more awesome than standing inside a great cathedral. Voices seemed to shout to me from the ruins—joyful, singing voices.

I thought, "King Tut, with all his worldly wealth and power, went out of this world into the darkness, not knowing what awaited him one second after death. But these Christians, who had nothing, fell asleep in the arms of Jesus. They knew he would gently wake them in their own room within the Father's house!"

SET THE EYES OF YOUR FAITH ON CHRIST

Now this faith I'm speaking of is not "pie-in-the-sky." It is active, alive in the here-and-now. Several crucial things begin to take place inside us when we set our eyes of faith on Christ. If we do not, we are bound to feel cut loose from our moorings in the day of the storm—for storms will surely come.

In this, I am reminded of a poignant story about Giuseppe Verdi, the great nineteenth-century composer of operas. He was conducting one of his magnificent productions before a full house, and almost from the opening moment things began to go terribly wrong. The soprano was too shrill; the string section not quite in tune. Nonetheless, he persisted.

When the final curtain fell, the audience rose to its feet, applauding. Roses pelted the stage around him. To Verdi, whose artistic genius was suffering horribly, the applause was worse than being hit with stones. Was this pity? Then, as his eyes swept the audience, he saw the face of the Italian master composer, Rossini. As their eyes met, Verdi felt an even deeper conviction because of the poor performance. There was no earthly consolation for Verdi that day because he had looked into the face of the master and knew that the master knew.

Nor is there consolation in today's philosophy, which says, "You only go around once. So live life with gusto!" I can think of no mind-set more tragic, hopeless, futile, and full of despair than that, because many of life's moments are anything but filled with "gusto."

When we set our eyes of faith on Jesus, however, we cannot help but see his heartfelt compassion for our plight. And we know we can "approach the throne of grace with confidence, that we may receive mercy and find grace to help us in our time of need" (Hebrews 4:16).

More than consolation, we learn that Jesus has gone before to break through the barriers, preparing our way. Consider his night of turmoil in the Garden of Gethsemane when the Prince of Darkness was bearing down upon him and his own flesh was repulsed at the suffering just ahead. How did he make it through?

Certainly it wasn't because of the faithfulness of his companions. When Jesus yearned for human companionship, begging his disciples to stay awake and watch with him, they were a gross disappointment. Finally, he had to wake *them* and get them on their feet and moving before the soldiers came with their torches, spears, and ropes. But during those dreadful hours of agonized prayer, Jesus had readied himself by turning his face to heaven. What could he possibly have seen that would give him strength to face the coming horror?

We have a clue in Revelation chapter 4, where the Apostle John describes for us a sight that no other mortal eye has ever seen. He describes the marvelous throne of God, blazing with rainbow colors. Then he describes four living creatures, who represent all created beings, who stand on the sides of the throne. Also around the throne are twenty-four elders. Day and night, the living creatures sing, "Holy, holy, holy, Lord God Almighty!" And the elders reply, "You are worthy to receive glory and honor and power!" And so they sing, antiphonally, back and forth before the Lord as heaven resounds with their mighty voices.

This, I believe, is akin to what Jesus caught sight of in the garden. Paul tells us that he was caught up in "the joy set before him." And that was the joy of completing his Father's will.

John's description in Revelation reminds me of an uncanny experience my family and I had on a visit to the retreat center at Lake Junaluska, North Carolina. We don't hear much these days about "all-day singing and dinner on the grounds" as they used to call it. But we had one of those old-time gatherings at the Methodist retreat center there one evening.

When the preaching service was over, we expected it would close with a hymn, but there was a surprise. Half of the congregation, numbering about one thousand, was sent down to the near shore of the lake. The other half, about another one thousand people, went to the head of the lake, which happens to be at the foot of a mountain. On the side of that mountain stands a great, lighted cross, shining in the night.

The far-away half of the congregation began to sing, the words echoing toward us across the still lake water: "Amazing grace, how sweet the sound, that saved a wretch like me!"

And we echoed in reply: "I once was lost, but now am found—was blind, but now I see!"

Back and forth, resounding from the hillsides, the song rang. And I thought, with shivers up my spine, "This is the way heaven is going to be."

Yes, we *can* experience the joy set before us when we keep our hearts alive and moving toward God in worship. Paul reminds us elsewhere to be filled with the Spirit continually: ". . . singing and making melody to the Lord with all your heart, always and for everything giving thanks in the name of our Lord Jesus Christ to God the Father" (Ephesians 5:19–20). When we do, our souls resonate with that heavenly chorus, and we follow that sound of singing that draws us onward through all our hardships. Faith enables us to hear its distant sound of triumph.

WE *ARE* GOING TO WIN

It's not just that we want to emulate Christ and somehow to keep an "otherworldly" smile on our lips in the face of adversity. We have the "home field advantage" because we have the inner *conviction* that we are going to win.

We Christians often think that ours is the age of unbelief. Truly, we do face doubt and despair at every hand. Not long ago, I overheard a man say to his friend, "Look, don't share any more of your doubts with me. I have enough of those. I need some affirmations!" But others who have gone before us have faced worse skepticism and paid higher prices for their faith.

Paul, who faced hardship, ridicule, and rejection gave us the secret of his ability to overcome all things. He declared that he could be joyful in trials "for I know whom I have believed, and I am sure that he is able to guard until that Day what has been entrusted to me" (2 Timothy 1:12).

From the first century, when Christians faced dreadful opposition to their faith, comes yet another story of faith that triumphed. I have read of one humble believer who was hauled before a vicious judge. Again and again the judge attacked the man's faith and tried to make a mockery of his testimony but could not.

Finally, with great sarcasm, the judge sneered, "Do you think the likes of you could stand in the presence of an Almighty God?"

The Christian responded gently, "I do not think. I *know* that I will stand in the presence of my Redeemer and my God."

For many through the ages, Christianity has been a "think so" religion. Today, too, many enlightened, educated folks are leery of accepting the claims of Scripture. After all, they say, don't other religions also claim that they are the only way? And so, tossed by winds of doctrine, conflict, and doubt, their Christianity becomes a weak philosophy with nothing certain about it.

But the Christian faith is not a "think so" religion. It is a hope that became a certainty when Jesus "passed through the heavens" to stand before God on our behalf. We may doubt ourselves sometimes. We may feel bewildered and not understand much of the conflict and suffering in our world. But we *know* whom we have believed. That is the conviction we accept from Paul and that great cloud of witnesses, like a relay runner grasping a baton.

The Christian faith is not a "think so" religion. It is a hope that became a certainty when Jesus "passed through the heavens" to stand before God on our behalf.

With these Christians, and all believers down through the ages, you and I also know that we are headed to a better, more beautiful place. There, Christ himself will wipe away every tear from our eyes. We know that we will someday cross that barrier to an eternal home where pain and death are no more. Then, the Bible says, we shall see him as he is—and we shall become *like* him (see 1 John 3:2).

And *that* will be the ultimate reshaping for every one of us. All of our struggles will end. All of the things we have tried to change in ourselves will be done in an instant, as Paul says, "in the twinkling of an eye." At last, we will be fully in the hands of the Master Craftsman, like gold that has been passed through the many, many fires of life. We will know the joy of purity.

Have you ever been tempted, in the face of hardship or loss or pain, to doubt? Then listen to the Apostle Paul,

> Who shall separate us from the love of Christ?
> Shall tribulation, or distress, or persecution, or famine, or
> nakedness, or peril, or sword? . . .
> No! . . . neither death, nor life . . . nor anything else
> in all creation, will be able to separate us from the love of God
> in Christ Jesus our Lord!
>
> (Romans 8: 35, 37–39)

That is the kind of conviction our heavenly Father wants you to have as you continue on the journey that is set before you today. You can be completely certain that he is *for* you.

No matter what the challenge, the win is yours. You can be transformed from within. You have the home field advantage.